Here and Hereafter

The Eternity Connection

A Spiritual Memoir told in Short Stories

Joy Ibsen

STRATTON
——PRESS——
Publishing Life

HERE AND HEREAFTER
Copyright © 2021 **Joy Ibsen**

All rights reserved. No part of this book may be used or reproduced by any means, graphic, electronic, or mechanical, including photocopying, recording, taping or by information storage and retrieval system without the written permission of the author except in the case of brief quotations embodied in critical articles and reviews.

Stratton Press Publishing
831 N Tatnall Street Suite M #188,
Wilmington, DE 19801
www.stratton-press.com
1-888-323-7009

Because of the dynamic nature of the Internet, any web addresses or links contained in this book may have changed since publication and may no longer be valid. The views expressed in the work are solely those of the author and do not necessarily reflect the views of the publisher, and the publisher hereby disclaims any responsibility for them.

ISBN (Paperback): 978-1-64895-356-9
ISBN (Ebook): 978-1-64895-357-6

Printed in the United States of America

For Diane
all the Best.

[signature]
1/20/2023

To Mathias, Karen Ann, Sofus, Frances, Willis, Borge, Andy, Herb, Jack, Nelly, Martin, Herald, Ozzie, Jens, Miss Miller, Marie, Roxanne, Father Gordon, Damian, Laura, Max and Minnie, Asta, Charlotte, John Mitchell, and Socrates, the major characters in this book who now live in the hereafter, thank you for what you contributed to my life, to the here and now and to the future!

and

To the readers who are creating their own spiritual legacies, Enjoy the journey!

CONTENTS

PREFACE

Entering into what is surely the final quarter of my life is like getting to the end of a really good novel and finding out what happens to the characters, including me. There are many surprises—things turn out better than expected. Life is great! Life is meaningful. Life is a series of stories.

Spiritual legacy is perhaps the most significant aspect of this book. When I look back at the family into which I was born, I remember the stories of a spiritual nature that deeply affected the very core of my being. We did not talk much about these stories, but we knew them. These powerful stories could pull us through any challenge, any heartbreak, any doubt. They are stories about death and new life.

One was my father's story of the experience he had during the Depression when he was hitch-hiking and riding a freight train to his first job as a minister in Oakland, California. (The full story is told in *Unafraid, Life Lessons: Sermons to Live By and Tales of Listeners Learning to Live Unafraid.*) In the Rocky Mountains—hungry, nearly broke, and very hot, Harald Ibsen walked the highway, but because of a recent murder, he was not picked up by passing cars. He also was grieving because he had received a telegram from Denmark that his mother had died. He would never see her again. Filled with self-doubt, physically tired, and discouraged, he sat down in despair on a rock by a mountain stream. He listened to the mountain stream; it seemed to speak in words, *"I can overcome all hindrances and obstacles on the way to my destination because I have power behind me—you can do the same."* These words carried him through the next forty years of his ministry and life.

My mother, Asta Ibsen, depressed and deep in grief following the death of her baby boy Paul had an urge to leave the Minnesota parsonage and go to her baby son's nearby grave. There, in the bleak cold wintertime, she was astonished to find a beautiful flower miraculously growing on Paul's little grave. My mother was filled with peace; she knew her baby boy was fine, perfectly fine! She was able to go on with life, to enjoy and celebrate life again.

Such stories mean life is about more than we know! Spiritual forces of ultimate goodness are at work and available to us. No matter what life hands us, we are able to experience grace and goodness.

When present reality is intertwined with glimpses of the eternal, we are taught something of the nature of ultimate reality. We realize what is most important in life. Life keeps getting better! We begin to see curious connections between people and events, synchronicities. As I wrote this book, I saw connections in life happenings I had never seen before.

Once, the topic of death was something we rarely discussed. Now we need to have more conversation about life-endings—death, afterlife, and even before life. One of the best ways to accomplish this is through stories—real stories—with people who can hear and receive what we have to say. I have shared my stories on the following pages. I hope you find them meaningful and that you will share your own stories and create your own spiritual legacy.

—Joy Ibsen
July, 2020

INTRODUCTION

I did not intend to write a memoir; I intended simply to write real life stories about death and life, but when I placed them in a linear sequence, I realized it was about my own life experiences and two major questions: What happens after death? What on earth are we doing here?

Life-endings come differently—sometimes too quickly, at other times with agonizing slowness—whether a result of illness, accident, violence, errors in judgment, suicide or simply old age. Is a particular life-ending a matter of fate or simply accidental? Is it God's plan, our plan, or no plan? What do we know about the *hereafter?* The before-life? What happens to those we love after they die? Do they still care for us? Influence us?

The Quaker philosopher Rufus Jones described death as a "hatching—changing from one form into another." *Here and Hereafter* focuses on other related "hatchings"—transformations experienced by the observer, comforter, caregiver, witness, griever. An ever-deepening understanding of life and life-endings often comes from witnessing "hatchings," whether shocking, grievous, welcome, or absolutely amazing.

Grief is real. The loss of a loved one can seem overwhelming, but at such times, we have an opportunity to perceive a reality beyond our usual abilities. Such moments may be called *kairotic*—a Greek word that refers to an in-breaking of God's eternity into time. Mortality and eternity come together, and major changes can occur. We may have new insights resolving what seemed impossible, be inspired to follow a new direction in life, experience the eternal.

I prefer to use the compound word *life-ending* rather than death as much as possible. The word *death* is associated with doom, gloom, finality, fear, futility, powerlessness—the enemy. We need to look at death in a different way—the necessary endings of individual lives. Life leads to death. Each marvelous chapter in creation's magnificent story has a conclusion. While it is natural for life to end, *Life*, with a capital *L*, continues! Life leads to death, but death also leads to life.

Background Statement

I was raised as a minister's daughter in the American (Danish) Evangelical Lutheran Church of America. Considered the more progressive of Lutheran churches, it was founded by N. F. S. Grundtvig (1783–1872), the Danish thinker, educator, politician, nation-builder, hymn writer, and founder of the folk schools. Unfortunately, most people in the United States know very little, if anything, about him. However, my life has been shaped by his values, and I continue to explore and study his work because I believe he speaks directly to contemporary needs. Briefly, Grundtvig believed in "a simple life, a merry heart." *Enjoy life* is the mantra that includes an active life of dancing, exercise, singing, and lifelong learning. "Human First, Christian comes next" is a Grundtvigian slogan. One need not be Christian or any other religion to be a good person. Ethical behavior is possible from simply being human. "The living word" is more important than the written word. The Bible, a holy book containing great wisdom, is not to be taken literally. Grundtvig was strongly committed to freedom of thought, and his legacy includes a profound spirituality that embraces the secular world.

Walter Capps (1934–1997) University of California, Santa Barbara, professor-theologian and US congressman summarized Grundtvigian values as (1) affirmation of human life, (2) staying as close to nature as possible, (3) belief in the beauty and goodness of ordinary life, and (4) commitment to lifelong learning.

Here and Hereafter reflects principle 3—the beauty and goodness of ordinary lives. While the book includes the deaths of two famous people, it is the greatness of wonderful ordinary people who make life worth living.

I attended divinity school at the University of Chicago in the early 1960s, when the short-lived "God is Dead" theology was at its height. The phrase simply meant that the "old-man-in-the-sky-god," with his elaborate, all powerful, micromanaging system of rewards and punishments, is an outdated idea. While the death of God as a Super Being has turned out to be an unpopular concept, it has led many people to new understandings of creation, the divine and the eternal. While I loved divinity school (I was fortunate enough to have two classes with Paul Tillich) and had a full scholarship, I dropped out after one year to make it economically possible for my husband to attend graduate school, a prefeminist tradition. When asked why I was going to divinity school, I would answer that I wanted to become divine. How foolish of me! You and I, all of us, are already divine!

My understanding of God is, first and foremost, found in the teachings of Jesus. However, I am gratefully influenced by other religions, including Buddhism, Judaism, Hinduism, Native American teachings, and Indian mysticism. There will never be another person like either me or you—never. But I have no doubt about the reality of the hereafter. Reincarnation? Not as usually interpreted, but I see it as a possible form of spiritual recycling and continual learning. Each person is an exquisite individual spirit dwelling within a unique combination of DNA, environment, experience, and cellular memory living in community with other exquisite individual spirits. Each birth is a new opportunity for growth. Life continues and continues. The soul never dies. We are part of a whole.

Connecting the Dots

Here and Hereafter consists of a series of real-life stories, connecting the dots between experiences relating to the life-endings of people important to me. It is divided into four age-related sections:

Part I—Confronting Life-Endings (Childhood)
Part II—Seeking Reasons (Adolescence)
Part III—Experiencing Other Dimensions (Adulthood)
Part IV—Acceptance, Integration, and New Beginnings (Maturity)

The chronicle begins with early childhood experiences, continues through self-conscious adolescence, is challenged by adult questioning of "why?" and finally arrives at a state of mind where the *hereafter* becomes more fully integrated into a wholeness. The stories are inspired by actual events told primarily in first person. When I lacked information concerning the details about a circumstance, I have, of necessity, imagined some details of the story. For privacy purposes, a few names have been changed. These stories represent reality as I perceive and understand it. Another person could have had an entirely different interpretation of the same event.

Paths of increasing awareness are not linear. At times, we may feel we are going backward. The need to confront an unexpected life-ending and questions of "why?" reoccur throughout our lives.

Many people are confused about the relationship between spiritual growth and religious growth. Individual spirituality blossoms through meditation and prayer. Religion is a group spiritual experience. Individual spiritual experiences can deepen one's religion. Religion can increase, complement, or stifle one's spirituality. Religion and spirituality should resonate with and support our life experiences. From time to time, we change our minds about what we believe as a result of what we encounter on our spiritual journeys. We seek new life experiences as a result of our spiritual growth. Our capacity to change and adjust are necessary, the fertile ground for individual and societal growth.

Here and Hereafter is a book of stories about the here—life on earth, and also about the hereafter— eternity, especially as glimpsed at times of death, and how they interconnect.

I think we are on the edge of new spiritual enlightenment, and we are experiencing immense upheavals that typically accompany great changes. We have made remarkable technological advances in the last two centuries, but it is possible, even necessary, that humanity will make remarkable spiritual advances in the coming centuries. Glimpses of the hereafter, now rejected by many, may soon be considered as elementary as the alphabet.

My hope is that *Here and Hereafter: the Eternity Connection* will lead to more enjoyment of here, a new conscious awareness of the hereafter, and new understandings about the connections between them. It is those interconnections that make life really fascinating.

A quotation from a Quaker philosopher:

I never go to a funeral without thinking of the miracle of transformation... In his own mysterious way, God has emptied the nest by the hatching method; all that was excellent, lovable and permanent in the one we loved has found itself in the realm for which it was fitted. (Rufus Jones)

From a paper found in my great uncle, Soren Rodholm's desk following his death:

"Thanatopsis"
November 28, 1940

This morning I had a strange experience. It was obviously more than a mere dream. It was as real to me as sitting here writing. I believe I was dead momentarily—how long, it is impossible to say. I stood by a running brook. The scene was sylvan and green. I followed the brook; it was more and more beautiful around me.

There was a deep, wide chasm. The brook widened into a river far away and it was lovely. I floated over the chasm, easily and unhindered. Everything grew more and more beautiful. I reached for the beauty: "Fill my heart!"—and it streamed into my soul. I wanted nothing better than to go on; but I had to return. I don't know why—I am writing this in case I should be found some day "dead of a heart attack." From my point of view, then, it would be a mighty and wondrous liberation. (SDR)

From "The Word," a hymn adapted by S. D. Rodholm from the works of N. F. S. Grundtvig:

> Only in the Word ascends
> Man beyond the life that ends:
> In the Word he breaks his prisons,
> Soars aloft to higher visions.
> Comprehends eternity.

From Mads Ibsen (1840–1901), my great grandfather, who immigrated to the United States in 1889, on his deathbed to his family gathered:

> I am not tired of life, in no way, but I am ready to go. I don't think I will be stored away until the day of judgment, so you might believe that I am with you when you get together.

When I was a child I spoke as a child I understood as a child I thought as a child; I reasoned like a child; but when I became a man [woman], I gave up childish ways. For now we see in a mirror dimly, but then face to face. Now I know in part; then I shall understand fully, even as I have been fully understood. So faith, hope and love abide; these three; but the greatest of these is love.

—1 Corinthians 13:11–13

PART I

Confronting Life-Endings

1

Mathias (Mah-tees')

Mathias was already an old man when I was born. As sweet as the honey from his honeybees, he was one of the gentlest, kindest gentlemen who ever lived. The Andersens, Mathias and his son, Iver, lived across the highway from my first home, the parsonage (no longer standing) in Diamond Lake, a small Danish community in southwest Minnesota. Since there is neither lake nor diamonds, one might question the reason for its name. My father told me it is was because the dew in the fields sparkles like diamonds, and long ago the fields were an ancient lake. While Diamond Lake might appear to be a nearly forgotten crossing on Highway 75, a perceptive person can still sense its ancient wisdom, a community still richer than diamonds.

In the early 1940s, when I was a toddler, the Andersen home had a fairytale garden with a statue of a *nisse* (Danish elf) who fished from a small pond bearing enormous water lilies. This delightful painted fellow with his green jacket, red cap, and white whiskers was surrounded by many unseen but real *nissemen.* You can always tell when little folk reside in a garden because the garden is pristinely neat but not at all severe. The little folk enable gardens to bloom, flowers to happily flourish. It is magical! Hollyhocks of softly vibrant colors talk to each other, tell jokes, argue good naturedly, admire one another with sincere compliments, and extend sympathetic good wishes in times of distress, such as the coming of hailstorms or high winds.

Mathias had a gazing ball by his pond. Unschooled in self-doubt at age 2, I enjoyed kissing my reflection on the silver globe in Mathias's garden while my brother David, who was three years older, pretended to catch fish alongside a *nisse,* both of them holding fishing poles with lines extended into the little pond. The thrill of my young life was to jump off Mathias's stone picnic table into his arms. With trustful anticipation, I would leave the solidity of the stone tabletop and shriek with delight as I jumped forward into nothingness. Mathias caught me in midair, spun me around once, twice, perhaps even three times. Feeling the tickle of Mathias's long beard and mustache as they brushed against my face with each spin, I enjoyed the pleasure of such a daring adventure without threat of unpleasant consequences. Mathias always caught me and saved me from falling. When it came to catching me, preventing a mishap, he was more reliable than God.

When I was four years old, Mathias died. By that time, we had moved to Iowa, but my parents returned to Diamond Lake for the funeral of their beloved friend and neighbor. Mathias's body (it seemed to me then that it was Mathias himself) was placed in a box (casket) on the unheated porch off the parlor, as if he were stored temporarily, like an apple pie when there is no room available in the refrigerator. My mother said Mathias was on the porch because it was cooler there, a statement that informed my uncluttered brain that dead people need to be kept cool. I had never seen a dead body before, and it made an impression on me, but a relatively slight one.

Mother took me by the hand out on the porch to see Mathias. My friend, my catcher, Mathias, lay still, lifeless. I looked dutifully at his body and watched a fly try to bother him. Mathias didn't mind it at all. The fly flew around his beard and landed on his vest. Mathias made no effort to brush the fly away. His familiar kindly slight smile was set a bit stiffly between his mustache and long beard. I instinctively understood that Mathias would never move again, never again catch me and whirl me around. But I was getting too big to jump off the picnic table and have someone catch me anyway. It was another ending—like the ending of a birthday party or a visit from my grandparents. Mathias's playing with me had stopped, and as much as I loved him, it seemed perfectly all right that it was over. I was a little sad, but more good times would come.

*****

More than six decades later, I stand by my infant brother's grave and contemplate all he has meant to me, this tiny baby who died after living only two months, who broke my parents' hearts but also strengthened them for living. On his small grave this late summer afternoon, a delicate planting of violet and yellow pansies barely bloom. Who is still caring for the grave so many years after Paul's family moved away?

Paul was called a blue baby—he had a hole in his heart between two chambers—which then could not be repaired. My father wanted him to be the last child, a sibling for my older brother, but a year and a half after Paul's life ended, I was born, and then my sister came three years later. All my life, I have struggled with the implications of owing my lifetime to Paul's death, until I realized I was making too much of it, using it as an excuse for my overachieving personality. Now mentally I send up a wordless prayer. Instantly there is a message in my brain: *Someday in this lifetime, you will meet Paul. You will be good friends. He will help you.*

Not wanting to break an unexpected moment of grace, embraced by the murmuring of the remaining elm trees left along the cemetery path, I exist in neither space nor time. Then, after a few seconds, I move to anticipation and excitement.

Finally, I turn and leave.

*****

For many years, it has been an annual ritual to visit the grave of my infant brother, who lies buried in the cemetery beside the Diamond Lake Church. When I visit the cemetery, I first stop to visit the graves of Mathias and his son, Iver, before going to see Paul's grave. Mathias's grave, marked with a very large prairie stone, is next to his wife's grave, a short distance from the church gate. Iver is buried nearby. Iver's widow lives across from the cemetery on Highway 75 in a pink stucco bungalow; for many years now, she has been the caretaker for the honey farm. One day, she will share Iver's tombstone, which bears an etching of a beehive. Wallentyne was once an attorney, a very attractive, athletic Polish woman whom Iver met on a train in Europe when he was nearly sixty years old; they were married long after Iver's bachelorhood seemed permanent to everyone in Diamond Lake. Wallentyne left her home and family in Poland and moved to Minnesota to work alongside him. There she learned to make championship honey and continue the Andersen family tradition long after Iver was gone.

Having completed my pilgrimage to the cemetery, I cross the highway to see Wallentyne, the daughter-in-law Mathias never knew. At the front of a winding driveway lined with huge pink and ruby hollyhocks is a little hut with various sizes of jars of honey and a sign: "Take the Honey: Leave the Money." Compared to previous years, there are only a few jars and only about $3 in the small bowl. I proceed to the back door of the house, through the garage, and knock at the door.

It is a hot afternoon and a long time since Mathias died, when I sit in the living room with Wallentyne, who alights on the rocking chair like a slender aging butterfly, occasionally flying around the room as she chatters, exuding her dedication to honey, cinnamon, and swimming in cold water. Wallentyne goes to the kitchen and brings refreshing health drinks before alighting once more. The house, now decorated with Polish dolls and bright-colored paintings on black velvet rather than the former soft blue Danish figurines, reflects Wallentyne's vibrant spontaneous energy. The ancient cob stove in the kitchen, the oak table and chairs in the dining room remind me of Iver and Mathias, as does the bee colony near the bay windows, a hive from which bees can fly freely into and out of the house. With her permission, I open one side of the wooden box and peer through the glass wall. Wallentyne points out the queen bee, and I watch the amazing construction of their honeycomb.

"I am so glad to see you, darling girl. I loved your mum. Your mum was so wonderful. She always came to see me," Wallentyne recalls the time so long past it seems like a forgotten dream. Suddenly I miss my mother with an almost painful sharpness. She should be here with me."

"They were great friends," I say, "Mother and Iver."

"Yes, they were. I know you miss your mum. I miss my mum. Every year, before she died, I went to Poland to see her—every year as long as she lived. Now I still go, but my mum…is gone. Still I go and see my family. And I go to her spa in Poland for a month. See how well I am? It is from the honey and from cold water. At the spa, I sit in water day after day. Cold water. Here, I swim every morning. No matter how cold it is."

"Where do you swim?"

"In the lake."

"Lake Benton?"

"Yes, it is a beautiful lake. Beautiful! I swim every day. Some say Lake Benton is too cold. The water is not too cold. In Poland, we always swim in cold water. Here! Have some honey with cinnamon. Cinnamon is very good for you! Here! I show you." Wallentyne bounces up, then out into the kitchen, returning with typed instructions detailing the healthy aspects of cinnamon. I reach for one of the crackers she has prepared, generously coated with honey and cinnamon, and vow to eat more of each. Wallentyne looks terrific.

Among piles of books and picture-covered walls, we sit, Wallentyne and I, drinking honey-cinnamon-vinegar water. Handsome in her late seventies, Wallentyne, wears a thin, short nightgown to keep cool. She has been working in the barn harvesting honey. Pulling up the skirt of her capricious nightgown, barely covering her muscular thighs, she laments, "Television, it is awful! Sex. Sex. Sex. Oh,

31

it is so stupid." She pulls her nightgown higher up, mocking a sexy pose.

I laugh and nod.

"I won! I won second place in the whole country with my honey. All by myself! I should have won first. Only two points and I would have won first. But all by myself, I won it! Second is good. Right? Yes, second is very good. I took my prizes over to my boy, Iver [in the cemetery], and I said, 'Iver, look at this! See, my darling boy! See it. See how well I do! I did it all by myself! See, honey! My darling boy! Look! I did it!" She points her chin upward and lifts her hand as if to show me the invisible medal.

"That's fantastic!"

We sit together a few minutes. Past celebrations and triumphs disappear far too quickly.

"It is so awful now. Poison. Poison! No flowers. No bees. People poison the fields with fertilizer and pesticides!" We have talked about this each year I visit, and there seems no reprieve for either the flowers or the bees. Only more poison.

Wallentyne continues to lament, "I have lost all my boys now. Iver died. They killed John." (John was Wallentyne's second husband whom she married and who lived with her on the honey farm after Iver died.) "The hospital killed him."

I nod, not wanting to hear the story again—how John was given the wrong medicine. Much of my working life has been spent in hospitals. Cures can sometimes kill, but I don't want to talk about it.

Wallentyne suddenly brightens as if to please me. "But I have kept Iver's name. Wallentyne Andersen. I would not do that to Iver. But John… John was a good boy too. A good boy!"

"Yes, he was." I mentally visualize the bow-legged, bald-headed, crippled-with-arthritis man. Wallentyne first cured John's dog, a boxer, with gallons of honey and vinegar. enabling him to walk on all fours again; then Wallentyne cured John, enabling him to walk and marry her.

I look at the doorway to the porch, something I do whenever I am visiting. "I remember when Mathias died. I was a little girl. It was the first time I saw someone who had died. He was in a coffin on the porch."

"You remember that? Yes, yes, that's the way they did it then. I never knew Mathias. I wish I had. Now everyone is gone except me." She shrugs her shoulders, and her whole body moves. "Just me, Wallentyne. Iver and his brother, Hans, are gone. And Hans's wife. She died right after Hans, and now Carl. A terrible boy. Everyone…gone!"

I set my cracker down on the plate. "Carl died?" (Carl was Iver's nephew and my age.)

"You know him? You know Carl?"

"Yes, a little," I say, remembering the handsome young man I had met in Berkeley several years ago. "What happened to him?" Carl should have carried on—something of Mathias and Iver!

"What do you call it?" She searches for an English word, an explanation. Unable to locate it, she twists her body into a mockingly feminine posture.

"AIDS?" I ask, surprised.

"Yes, yes, that's it. AIDS. He came here once, but he was an awful boy. They spoiled him. Now, no one is left."

I recall the plaque on the outside of the Chicago hospital entrance where I worked, a recognition that the busy land on which the hospital is built once was a Native American village, a daily reminder of impermanence.

Again, I look at the doorway to the porch and remember Mathias. I feel as if again I am four years old, gazing at Mathias's dead body, no, not at Mathias, but at the silver gazing ball at the pond by the *nisser*. It is as if the silver sphere swirls through time, spinning backward—before Wallentyne, before Carl, before AIDS, before Iver and Mathias, before there were highways and churches—back and back, swirling to when Dakotans roamed the beautiful unspoiled prairie and quarried pipestone from sacred land.

Suddenly, like time, the gazing ball stops and begins to fly in the opposite direction—moving fast-forward from the ancient lakes to the era of the sacred pipestone, swirls past epochs of gravel roads and white country churches, whirls past Mathias, Iver, and Carl, reels on through the ages, on and on, past Wallentyne and me and everyone I know, continues spinning, twisting, rotating, expanding toward—what?

Who will come next? Anyone? Will the honeybees or earth survive another millennium? Who will be here when no one takes the honey and leaves the money, when there is no pipestone left to quarry, when Highway 75, the Diamond Lake Lutheran Church, the little cemetery, the pink stucco house, the honeybees and hollyhocks, perhaps even the *nissemen* are gone?

Just as when I looked at Mathias's body on the porch that afternoon so long ago, I am only slightly sad, because I know as I knew then there will be good times to come—more life-endings. And more life- beginnings.

2

Karen Ann

My mom was washing clothes in the basement when the telephone rang, so I climbed up on our big brown studio couch and standing on my tiptoes, unhooked the ear phone. Two large bells on the telephone box stared back at me like bulging black eyes. Holding the ear-horn close to my ear, I took a deep breath and bravely talked into the speaker. "Hello."

"Hello, dear." It was Karen Ann's mother. "Let me talk to your mom," she said.

"Okay. I'll get her." I jumped off the couch. Karen Ann was coming to play that afternoon. Maybe her mother was calling to ask what time they should come. I hoped she wasn't calling to say they weren't coming. It might rain, but we could play inside.

My mom was putting wet clothes through the wringer of the washing machine so she could hang them in the basement. When she saw me on the steps, she stopped the wringer.

"Mama, Karen Ann's mom is on the phone."

"I'll be right up," she said, reaching for a towel to wipe her hands.

Mama hurried up the basement stairs and picked up the phone. I listened carefully. "I'll let Harald know," Mama said. "I'm sure he'll want to go to the hospital." Mama turned to me when she hung up.

"Karen Ann is sick. They are taking her to the hospital in Harlan."

She must really be sick if they were taking her to a hospital, which meant she wasn't coming to play. I felt bad. Often we would play Snow White. Karen *looked* like Snow White, with her straight dark brown hair and the big bow she usually wore on the back of her head. Her eyes were also brown, not blue like mine. When we played Snow White and Rose Red, I was always Rose Red. Today, I had all my paper dolls ready. If it rained, we could have made a house by spreading blankets over the sides of the dining room table and chairs.

Sometimes I went to Karen Ann's house to play. She lived on a farm with a barn full of animals—kittens, cows, pigs, and a bunch of horses. Sometimes her dad let us play in the hayloft and jump in the hay.

It rained all day. My mom hung up clothes in the basement. My little sister Karma and I made a playhouse under the dining room table and chairs. We played with our paper dolls, and she was careful with them, but we didn't have a very good time.

My dad, a minister, opened up the doorway of our playhouse to tell us he was leaving to visit Karen

Ann in the hospital. I couldn't go because I was just a kid. When he came home, I was playing with our dog, Boots, on the studio couch. Boots, a Boston bulldog, had a funny smell, maybe like Boston. My dad sat down beside me.

"I saw Karen Ann at the hospital," he said. "She has what is called a bad appendix. It is inside her body right here." He pointed to the side of my stomach. "They will fix it tomorrow morning. The doctors will operate, cut out the part that's making her sick, and she will be good as new in no time." He stood up, but turned to say, "She said to be sure and greet you."

That night before I went to sleep, I prayed, "Now I lay me down to sleep…" At the end, I added, "Make Karen Ann well so she won't be sick anymore."

The next morning, I was jumping on the couch in my pajamas when my dad came downstairs. It was Sunday morning and almost time to get ready for Sunday school.

"Stop! Stop," he said, so I sat down, and he sat next to me. He was quiet for a moment and took a big breath. "I have some sad news," he said. "Karen Ann died last night." I looked at him and did not say anything. His eyes had a funny color, almost no color at all, like the color of rain.

"The infection she had inside her was worse than the doctors realized," he said. "Her appendix broke open during the night before they could operate, and they could do nothing for her. I'm…sorry," he said.

"She won't be coming over anymore?" I asked.

"No."

"Did she go to heaven?" I thought Daddy should have told me that she had gone to heaven.

"Yes," he said. "Yes, she did."

"Can she write to me?" Karen Ann was a second grader and knew how to write a lot of words.

"No. She won't be able to write to you."

I turned my face to the wall and hugged my dog, Boots, so tight he whimpered.

"Can I stay home from Sunday school? I don't feel very good," I said.

To my surprise, Daddy nodded.

* * * * *

The next day, my mom told me to put on my Sunday shoes and a dress because we were going to visit the Hansens. I was surprised. Why were we going to Karen Ann's house if she wasn't there?

On the way to the Hansens' farm, my dad liked to pretend there was a troll underneath the bridge over a creek. Usually we joked about it, but when we came to the bridge, no one said anything about it. Mama looked out of the window.

"I can't believe she's gone," Mama said. "I feel so sorry for them. Their only child. I can't imagine what they are going through. What can I say to them?"

"You don't need to *say* anything," my dad said.

I had thought we would be the only ones there, but the farmyard was filled with cars. We got out and walked past the pump and through the gate to the farmhouse. Karen Ann's dog, Trofast was barking. He came up to me, pressing his nose on my leg; I petted him behind his ear. Trofast, which means "faithful friend," wagged his tail.

Inside the back porch, I could smell fresh coffee. There were lots of women in the kitchen talking and fussing over the food, like they were having a party. But when Karen Ann's mother saw me, she began to cry. Then she made some awful sounds—like a wolf howling. One of the women came over and hugged her, but she cried even harder. Then some of the other women began to cry along with her. Mama put her hands on my shoulders and quickly led me, almost shoved me out of the kitchen. I looked back at Karen Ann's mother, who was crying and saying stuff I could not understand.

Why were all those women acting like babies? If Karen Ann was all right, they wouldn't be making a fuss like they were. She must not be in heaven. Something worse must have happened than what people would say. They weren't telling me the truth, for sure, just because I was a kid.

My mom took me into the living room and motioned for me to sit on a footstool by my father. "Just stay here for a little while. I'll be back," she said. I sat down by my dad. I watched her go back to the kitchen.

Sunlight was flashing through the lace curtains, making funny light patterns on the flowered carpet. I sat and watched the lights flicker on the rug and listened to the men talking as they sat in the scratchy overstuffed chairs, smoking their pipes or cigars. They didn't seem to notice me or even hear the women in the kitchen. From the footstool, I looked up at Daddy. The men were saying we needed warmer weather for the crops to grow. Men always talk about weather—how we need more rain or more sun. I liked being with them—the quiet, the smell of the smoke. I did not want to be like the women in the kitchen who cried like babies, even howled. I decided right then and there that when I grew up, I would stay away from kitchens. I would be like the men—quiet, safe in a haze of smoke.

A few minutes later, my mom came in, bent down, and asked me, "Do you want to go and see Karen Ann?"

"Is she *here*?"

Mama nodded.

I shook my head no.

Mama straightened up. "I think you should see her," she said.

"No!" I said.

She hesitated for a moment and then said, "All right. I'll go in first."

I hoped that would be the end of it and sat quietly listening to the men talk about raising turkeys. Then before I knew it, Mama was back.

"Come…come and see her. She looks like she's sleeping."

I looked at my mom. I saw no tears on her face.

"No!" I said, but I did not want the men to see me make a fuss, and in a way, I wanted to see what Karen Ann looked like now that she was dead.

"Come with me," my mom said. "Come." She took my hand.

Mama opened the door to Karen Ann's parents' bedroom, just as our neighbor Mr. Jensen and his wife were leaving. They both looked at us, but did not say anything. Mr. Jensen shook his head.

I was scared.

My mom held my hand and almost pulled me into the room, then led me toward the side of the bed with its huge carved headboard. We had played in that room once, Karen Ann and I. Her mother said we could play in there if we didn't jump on the bed.

I had my head down and was standing back so far I almost touched the flowers in the wallpaper. Finally, I lifted my head to see her.

A large purple veil was draped from the ceiling to the foot of the bed. Karen Ann lay under the veil like she really was a princess. Her head rested on a pillow. It was just like Mama had said—she looked like she was sleeping, sleeping alone in her parents' great big bed. She looked like…like Snow White.

I took a step closer. I looked as hard at her as I could, but I could only see that my friend Karen Ann lay under the purple veil, so quiet and still that she could never play with me or anyone else again. But I also knew Karen Ann was okay. No matter how hard her mother cried or what anyone said or did, I knew it. Karen Ann was just fine.

* * * * *

Later—almost thirty-five years later—I sat alone in a gray room in a Moscow hotel trying to be grateful, while my fellow travelers on a workshop tour were undoubtedly enjoying a pleasant dinner in spite of communist regime restrictions. It was drab and lonely in the room, and I was feeling morose, weak, unable to walk more than a few steps, but I was still alive, having successfully communicated to Russian doctors, through pantomime, my deadly allergy to penicillin. Suffering from a severe kidney infection, I had been in pain and terrified when I was taken by ambulance to a Leningrad hospital; but in spite of my fear, the hospital experience had been a good one. I had shared a room with four fantastic Russian women, who in spite of repression, had rebuilt my faith in the human spirit. Through pantomime communication, we had become almost soul mates.

Luckily, I was given permission to leave the Leningrad hospital and was now recovering in Moscow. A shot of an alternative antibiotic in my rear haunch and some little white pills were defeating the infection, but the shot had made it difficult for me to walk.

A knock on the door. It was Gwen, our workshop leader, with supper on a tray. Gwen combined visits to countries throughout the world with self-development work for her students. Being in a foreign environment was helpful in changing life patterns, but the only change I was interested in at the moment was gaining strength. I looked at the colorless food in the colorless room and took a few bites of bland potatoes.

For a few minutes, we sat in silence. Then Gwen looked at me and asked, "What happened to you when you were young that made you so afraid of hospitals?" Gwen had a way of zeroing in on the real issue, which had totally eluded me. Gwen had been with me in Leningrad when I was hauled away by ambulance. In 1980 Russia, no one was allowed to accompany a foreigner to the hospital. I couldn't help but protest. Who wouldn't be afraid to go alone to a hospital in such circumstances, but my tears betrayed me; it was obvious there was something deeper.

"I don't remember," I said at first, but memories were stirring within my brain. I remembered Karen Ann! Why would I be remembering her now after so many years—before I grew up, worked, was married, and had children—way back to when I played with paper dolls?

"I did have a friend when I was a child." I said. "She was my best friend. "She…she died in the hospital. It was a long time ago." Surely, that wasn't what this was all about.

"What was her name?"

"Karen Ann. Karen Ann Hansen."

"Have you ever cried about losing your friend?" Gwen asked.

"No."

"Why not?" Gwen was kind but relentless.

"I don't know. At that time…at that time, it didn't seem like…like I should."

We sat a few minutes in silence as she waited for me to continue. "There was a visitation at the farmhouse. Her mother—no, several women were crying and carrying on in the kitchen. My mother took me into the living room to sit with the men. I-I wanted to be like them. They were calm, quiet. I didn't want to be like…like those hysterical women."

"And so you didn't cry."

"No, I-I didn't want to be like them." As I spoke, I began to realize the enormity of the choice I had made at age 6, and I began to weep. Once I allowed the tears, it didn't seem like I could stop. Gwen passed tissues to me. She had come prepared.

Finally, I managed, "I guess I failed, didn't I?"

"Failed at what?"

"Being calm like the men. I'm as emotional as… as any woman. Maybe worse. I just lock it up inside until it spills over."

"But she was your friend. Of course you were upset."

"It-it was…more than that. I didn't think she was going to die. My dad said she was going to be all right. I…I thought …I thought he and God, I don't know…had some kind of arrangement. He was a minister," I said.

"You were angry with your father?"

"Not angry, exactly, but my dad said that Karen Ann would be all right. I… I thought God would do what…whatever my dad asked."

"And when that didn't happen?"

"I guess I was…disappointed in him…and God." I began to sob.

"That's understandable," Gwen said. "Of course you were." She gave me a hug as I wept more tears away.

After Gwen left, I sat in silence a long time, looking out the window into the dull Moscow day.

I tried to recall details surrounding Karen Ann's life-ending. "Karen Ann said to greet you," my dad had said. I could hear him saying it, and while those were not words a little girl would say, I found them comforting. Did she say to tell me "hi"? Was it a kind of goodbye? Why had Karen Ann died? Was it her time? Had she accomplished what she came to do? Had she left for some other reason? Was it an accident? Were the doctors incompetent?

There were no answers. Only questions.

* * * * *

Two weeks later, back in the United States and happily reunited with my children, I wrote a long letter to my older brother, David, telling him how I had finally mourned for Karen Ann, and how the decisions I made at the time she died had shaped my personality.

My brother wrote back:

> You've got it all wrong. I remember it very differently. Karen Ann's father was so distraught that he was

suicidal. Dad was up all night with him. And I'll never forget Sunday School that morning. You must not have been there. We all knew Karen Ann had died, and everyone was waiting to see what Dad would say during devotions that morning. He came in looking exhausted. Everyone was quiet. He looked at us before he started to speak. I don't remember what he said, but in the middle of it he stopped, his voice broke, and he looked right at us. "I don't know why God would take a beautiful little girl like that," he said. His eyes filled with tears and he turned and left the room. It was the only time in my life I saw Dad cry. The other boys in Sunday School looked at me like, as if to say, "See your Dad's not so tough. He doesn't know everything." But I was proud of Dad, even if he did cry. I was glad he didn't say some baloney about being up with the angels. Someone told me that Karen Ann died because she ate some hair in her food. I know that is stupid, but to this day, I have a phobia about hair in my food.

I set down my brother's letter and sat on my bed, staring out into the vacant field in back of our condominium on the outskirts of Milwaukee. A key life-forming decision, one I had made as a child, was built on false assumptions; it was based on incomplete information. The plain truth is men hurt as much as women. I had constructed my personality on a faulty cornerstone, a misunderstanding that persisted, and explained a lot about my personality. I am very calm during a crisis until my emotions erupt. The women's movement came just in time for me. I needed a career; I needed to be emotionally distant, like men—to be independent. It was all a misunderstanding, one that backfired. Now it seemed too late to change. What can I do now? It's too late to change. Or is it? Perhaps I can explore some alternatives.

As I sat there a while longer, I recalled what it felt like to hold my mother's hand while looking at Karen Ann, bidding her farewell. As if the strength of my mother were still providing me with courage, I took one last look at Karen Ann under the purple veiling and knew in the deepest part of my soul that Karen Ann was—*is* fine. Absolutely fine. Asleep like Snow White, except, she would have awakened long ago.

Karen Ann Hansen, 1939–1946

Karen Ann's fifth birthday party
L–R: David Esbeck, Connie Elmquist,
Karen Ann Hansen, Joy Ibsen,
Jimmy Jessen, Carl Rasmussen

3

Sofus

"A…" I could not make out the next word. "Sti…?"

"Stitch," my mother supplied.

"Stitch," I repeated, and then started over.

"A stitch in…time…saves…nine." That was it! As a second grader, I had successfully read one of the poster sayings on the Jacobsen's kitchen wall, slowly making out each word. It made no sense to me. "Nine what?" I asked.

"Nine stitches," my mom answered. "If I mend your sock when you first get a hole in it, I won't have to sew as many stitches as if we wait until the hole gets big."

I still did not understand. How would anyone know that sign was about holes in socks? I looked at another sign on the wall in Hertha's kitchen: *"A pen-ny saved is a penny…"*

"Earned." This time Hertha supplied the ending to the sentence. Hanging on walls throughout the

Jacobsen house were sayings, short sentences like this one. I loved reading them and trying to figure out what they meant. A lot of words come together to say something—like a puzzle. Because my grandfather was a school janitor, he had given me a whole stack of words printed on small yellow cards, words rescued from a wastebasket, words to make sentences.

The dog sat on the chair. Mother went to the store. Jane ate her food.

I tried another of Hertha's sayings.

"Time waits for no man." I could read all the words in that sentence!

"Or woman," Hertha laughed as she mashed the potatoes. She was making a farewell dinner for our family—my father and mother, sister, brother, and me—before we moved to South Dakota.

I didn't know what *that* sentence meant either, but I didn't ask.

"Can you read this one?" my mother pointed to another saying.

"He…who…cuts…his …" I did not know the next word, although it looked like I should.

"Own," my mother said.

"Own," I repeated, and started over again. "He who cuts his…own…wood is…"

"Twice," Hertha said, helping me before my mother would.

"Twice," I repeated.

I began again. "He who cuts his own wood is twice…warm."

"Warmed," Mom said.

Okay. Now I could read the whole sentence. "He who cuts his…own wood…is…twice warmed."

Mom decided to explain. "A man first gets warm from cutting wood. The work makes him sweat. Then he gets warm from the fire he builds! If you do your own work, you get more out of it."

"She who cooks her own food is twice cooked," Hertha said, pulling a large roast out of the oven. She laughed as she wiped her forehead from her brow.

"He who bakes his own bread is twice baked," Mom said as Hertha's husband, Sofus, came in the kitchen door, and the two women laughed. Slightly bent over, Sofus was our town baker. He baked the best bread in Iowa. "What is going on here?" he asked.

"We're helping Joy read," Hertha answered.

I left the kitchen and climbed up the stairway to the bathroom on the second floor. Along the wall all the way to the top of the stairs, there were sentences shouting to me as if to say, "READ ME IF YOU CAN!"

"Don't row out fur…th…er…"—I did not know that word—"than you can row back."

I opened the door into the bathroom and looked around. There was a saying on every bathroom wall. "It's late—la-ter…than you think," I read. I knew the word *later*. I sat on the toilet and tried to make out the meaning. "It's later than you think." Maybe it was like when it was after eight or even nine o'clock at night and I had to go to bed before I was ready. I reached for the toilet paper.

* * * * *

A few weeks later, we moved to South Dakota to a town named Viborg, where long ago, my great-grandfather had settled and where we still had relatives. My father had always said he would not serve a congregation where relatives lived, but he changed his mind because the congregation had been without a minister for a year. Dad loved the South Dakota air, which he said was different from Iowa air. I didn't want to move. I liked our home in Kimballton, Iowa. My friend Elsa's home was by the brickyard and a junkyard! It was fun to race our bikes around stacks of bricks and hunt for stuff in the junkyard. Once I found an old doll, and we played hospital. Living in South Dakota would not be as much fun. The Iowa air was good enough for me, and I didn't want to move where I didn't know anyone. Elsa, the brick-yard, and the junkyard were a long way from South Dakota.

But soon it would be my eighth birthday. I loved my birthday being on April 1st because people always had fun and it was spring! I would get presents, and for the first time, kids from my new school would be coming to my birthday party. There would be cake and ice cream and games. Having a birthday on April 1st meant people made up jokes and played tricks on me, but I didn't care. I liked jokes. April Fool's Day is the best day in the year next to Christmas and Fourth of July, which doesn't come for a long time.

But a few days before my birthday, I heard my parents talking very quietly in the kitchen, and I knew something was wrong. "Something very bad has happened," my mother said. "Sofus Jacobsen died. He had a heart attack. The work in the bakery must have been too hard on him."

I did not know what to say. I thought of "Little Ejner" and his big sister Ingrid. Now they would not have a father. Little Ejner was a year older than I was. The only reason they called him Little Ejner was because he had an Uncle Ejner, who was a tall grown-up. When we had our moving-away dinner with the Jacobsens, Little Ejner had made a big fuss because he did not like his food mixed together, so his mother gave him a plastic plate with ridges so he could keep his peas out of his potatoes and gravy. Little Ejner was bigger than I was, but he still needed a father.

"Dad is going back for the funeral," Mom said. "They don't have a minister yet. It will be a very large funeral. Everyone knew Sofus. Everyone liked him. He will really be missed."

I thought of the smell of bread and rolls and pastries in Sofus's bakery. We didn't even have a bakery in South Dakota. In Sofus's bakery, there were stacks of pastries in a glass case that looked like jewelry. I loved the smell of fresh baked bread and pastries, which you could smell as soon as you came close to the bakery; it smelled so wonderful! Mother had told me Sofus got up at four o'clock in the morning to bake bread. What would happen to the Danish bakery without him? Who else would get up so early?

Then I understood the sign I had seen in the Jacobsen bathroom! I knew what it meant! It *is* later than we think! When we were at the Jacobsens', it was *later* than Little Ejner or his sister Ingrid, or Hertha or Sofus or anyone knew! *Later* was like something playing hide-and-seek, hiding and then surprising you, except it wasn't a good surprise. All those words, all those sayings in their house, meant something important! But how does anyone know *what* is later than we think? We *didn't know.* It is like a trick. Almost like an April Fool's joke, except not funny, more like Halloween.

"Unfortunately, your dad will miss your birthday. You understand," Mother said.

I looked at my dad. I could not believe he was going to miss my birthday. He knew I was going to be eight years old! But from the way my mother looked at me, it was clear that I was dangerously close to being selfish, so I nodded.

"I'll be back the day after your birthday," my dad said. "Save me some cake."

After my birthday? What good would that be?

I nodded again and thought, *It's later than they think.*

4

Frances

"It's starting to melt. I don't think we should cross," Edward said, a bit wearily, knowing it was unlikely his older sister would listen to him. Edward didn't want Frances to think he was a chicken, but he *was* worried. Besides, before school that morning, their mother had said, "Don't take the shortcut! The ice isn't safe this time of year. Go the long way. Promise!" She had looked at him intently as she helped him put on his boots. Frances had already headed out the door on her way to their country school and did not hear her mother.

Now on their way home, when Frances turned down the shortcut road, Edward tried to protest. "Mama said—"

"Oh, don't worry about it," Frances responded. "C'mon. Let's play 'Follow the leader.' You can be the leader if you want."

Soon they were at the creek, and Edward was even more worried. Maybe his mother was right.

Even though it would be a long walk back to the road and they would be late coming home from school, he thought they should turn around. Frances was always brave and daring; Edward knew he should stand up to her. "Mama said not to cross the creek. I'm not going. Let's turn around," he said.

"Edward…" Frances pleaded. "C'mon. Don't be a chicken."

"I'm not going with you," he said, continuing to follow her. At the creek's edge, he managed to protest. "I'm not a chicken. The ice…the ice isn't safe."

Nestled in a valley between two hills by their farm, the creek appeared frozen, even though much of the snow had melted in an early thaw. Edward looked upstream for running water. Frances was already testing the ice with one of her boots. "See. It's fine."

"No, it isn't," Edward said, feeling his throat close. "It's starting to crack."

"It's not cracking."

"Yes, it is. It's cracking."

"It's just cracking a little bit. C'mon. We can make it."

"No."

"We'll go one at a time. I'll go first."

The two had crossed the creek a hundred times, but now—? Edward could feel the warmth of the early spring through his damp mittens. He wished the sun was not shining so brightly; he wanted to feel the cold chill of an early spring day on his face, but he could not.

Edward watched as Frances moved one step at a time. "Ed-ward," she said in her singsong way.

"I don't want to. I'm staying right here."

"Be a baby. Stay there." First, she had called him a chicken; now, she said he was a baby. He wanted to protest. He wasn't a chicken, and he wasn't a baby. He just didn't like to go against what he had promised his mother.

"Mama said not to cross the creek."

"Well, do you want to go all the way back, all the way around now? It's going to start getting dark."

"No…" he said lamely. He looked down at his galoshes. Frances was crossing the creek. He was afraid to watch her. The ice had cracked in a few places upstream.

He looked up just in time to see a giant zigzag of a crack break loose and spread over the wrinkled face of the aging ice. Edward could see water! "Come back!" he yelled.

"Edward," she said, with less confidence and a mere shred of terror in her voice, while maintaining the calm authority of an older sister, "I can't go back. I have to keep going now."

He looked at her in disbelief. Frances was standing in the middle of the creek. Suddenly, the other side began to break up too. Cracks were coming from all sides—*pop, crack*—making the eerie sounds of a giant bowl of cereal.

"Hurry!" he cried out to her. "Hurry, Frances!" His voice cracked; his stomach was in knots.

But Frances stood motionless.

"Hurry!" Edward cried. "Frances, hurry up!"

She stood frozen, looking at both sides of the creek. "Edward," she said softly, almost tearfully. "Help me."

"I…I…I can't."

Frances stared at him a moment. A torrent of escaping waters divided them, making it impossible for him to reach her.

"Hurry, Frances," he said, tearfully. "Please hurry! Hurry to the other side!"

Frances turned and looked at him desperately, realizing she had been wrong about the creek, and now there was nothing to do about it, but even now, she did not want him to know he had been right. Edward saw tears falling down her cheeks, and he was engulfed by his cowardice. Then she nearly screamed, "Help me, Edward! He…lp me!"

Edward knelt down, crawling out on the ice as far as he dared, feeling the cold beneath his snow pants. "Go for it!" he said, looking up at her. "I can't reach you. Get out of there. Hurry. Hurry up. Hurry before…"

She finally moved, stepping as quickly as she could to the other side of the creek as the ice on the creek peeled away behind her. Torrents of water escaped, nipping at her heels.

"Hurry, Frances. Hurry….hurry up!" he said, which was silly, because now she had to move slowly, carefully, deliberately. Frances was almost to the other side when the ice underneath her gave way.

A dog-like yelp…a muffled call…a cry or a howl…then strange gulping sounds. Some came from Edward; some from Frances as Edward's life companion, his second mother, his blessed sister, slipped below the ice. The last thing he saw was the top of her purple knit hat their mother had made for her. He stared where she had fallen through. Where was she? Where did she go? He couldn't see her at all.

"Frances," he cried. "Frances! Frances!"

But Frances was in the water under the ice. Edward lay down on the ice that remained, reaching out as far as he could. The ice began to separate beneath him. His clothes became sopped with frigid ice water, and now he was soggy through his underwear down to his skin. Edward had to make the decision of his life—whether a choice or a reaction, he would never know. Suddenly he was squirming and crawling backward to the shore as the water rushed in on his small body. Scrambling to his feet on the shore, he looked once more for a sign of Frances, and saw none. He turned and ran, yelling as loudly as he could, "Help! Help!" crying hysterically all the too long way to the road, all the way to the bridge, all the way to the white frame house.

"Help! Help! Frances….Frances went through the ice! Help! Help! Somebody come, help! Frances… Frances!…Somebody…Help!"

* * * * *

Mrs. Thomsen, a short square-shaped woman, invited Ida Mae, the oldest of the Petersen children into the mortuary. She had been surprised by the call. "I want…" Ida Mae had said. "I want to fix her hair. I want to fix Frances's hair for the funeral."

I probably should not allow it, the undertaker thought, but it seemed the right thing to do in this case. Funerals for children were always difficult. One of the few women undertakers in the state, Mrs. T., as she was called in town, understood Ida Mae's feelings. How the hair looked made so much difference, and the child's body was in good condition. The father had run down to the creek right away and been able to pull her body out downstream. The cold, of course, helped too.

"You are sure you want to do this?"

"Yes."

"And your mother says it is all right?"

"We want her to look…nice."

"All right then."

"She's right in here," Mrs. T. said. She brought Ida Mae into the room where Frances's body lay in a white casket ready for the funeral the next day.

Ida Mae was less sure than she pretended to be. Because of cheerleading practice, Ida Mae had not been home the afternoon her sister died, had been absent when they brought Frances, limp, blue, and icy, up to the farmhouse. In fact, Ida Mae had seen only one other dead body, her grandmother's, and that was a long time ago.

After a moment of looking straight ahead at a vase of artificial flowers across the room, Ida Mae finally looked down at her sister's body…so unusually still, so quiet. She thought of how fast Frances could run—she would have been great in high school track. The two sisters had often run through the pasture, racing each other between haystacks. She remembered when Frances was a newborn, and her mother had first let her hold her baby sister. Frances had seemed like a real live doll to Ida Mae, and from the beginning, she had cherished and loved her plucky little sister.

For her funeral, Frances was dressed in her Christmas dress, a dark green velvet with a white lace collar. Frances had loved that dress; she had been so excited—twirled and whirled around in it in the farm house parlor. Frances was always excited, always running around; she was not afraid of anything, which was the problem with Frances.

Ida Mae had brought a hairbrush and comb with her, and she bravely began to carefully, gently brush Frances's hair. She was shocked at how different it was now. Frances no longer could move away from the brush or say "ouch." Thankfully, there were no snarls. Mrs. T. had already taken care of that. Without a tear, Ida brushed one side of Frances's hair, at first afraid to touch her with the other hand, and then she did touch her, and it was all right. She brushed the other side of Frances's hair. But how to brush the back of her head?

She looked at Mrs. T.

"Let me help you," the undertaker said. Mrs. T. lifted Frances's body for a moment, and Ida Mae quickly brushed the hair on the back of her head, as if she must hurry so that Frances could once more rest. Mrs. T laid the child's body back down. Ida Mae lightly brushed both sides again, turning in the little wisps of blonde curls toward Frances's small freckled cheeks. Tears started to come, and Ida alternately brushed back tears with her left forearm as she brushed back Frances's hair with her right hand, curling the sides so they would match.

Ida Mae tried to speak, "Someone said…," but she had difficulty mouthing the words: "Does… Does…"

"Does the hair continue to grow?" Mrs. T asked the question for her.

Ida Mae nodded, her face stiffly holding in tears.

"Just…a little. Especially in one so young."

Ida Mae nodded. She finished up with the soft bangs. "She looked good in bangs," she said. "Okay, now?"

Ida Mae touched her sister's head ever so gently with her hand. "Goodbye, Squirrel," she said quietly. "Squirrel" had been Ida Mae's pet name for her little sister.

*****

Not one single person blamed Edward for his sister's death. His mother kept telling him, "Thank God, I didn't lose both of you. Remember that, Edward. Don't ever blame yourself."

It was because people kept saying that he was not to blame, that Edward became convinced that somehow he *was* to blame, or why would they keep saying it? Edward knew the truth—if he had refused to follow Frances and starting going the long way home, Frances would have joined him and still be alive. He should not have followed Frances to the creek, or maybe he should have gone first and turned around. They were going to play "Follow the Leader." She had said Edward could be the leader, but he didn't like being the leader.

For the rest of the school year, Edward dragged himself to their country school, walking alone, missing Frances so much his heart hurt every step of the way. He had trouble doing his homework and didn't even like recess. When his teacher Mrs. Burns pleaded with him to play tag or softball, he reluctantly joined the other kids; he hated trying to have fun when he didn't feel like it. Frances had been a better softball player than he was; she made a hit almost every time she was up to bat—sometimes a home run. Frances should be there. She should be playing instead of him.

When Edward awoke in the morning, he sometimes forgot that Frances had died; he would think she was still alive and then he would remember and feel like not getting out of bed. At home, everything seemed an unpleasant chore. The house was quiet, way too quiet. Edward's mother was given to fits of crying, and his father seemed touchy, even ill tempered. In the evening, Edward did his homework, because he didn't want to cause difficulty, but he hated it, and his grades were not good. He hated everything. He just wanted Frances back.

Finally, it was the last day of school. Edward would receive his report card at his school in the morning and then attend a final assembly in the afternoon of all the Turner County elementary school students from both country and town schools. All country schools were closing; it would be the very last day—forever—not only of Edward's country school but all the country schools in South Dakota. Next year, Edward would go to school in the nearby town of Viborg; he would ride a bus. Edward hated the thought of riding a bus every morning, but at least he wouldn't be walking to school alone anymore. His parents said it was time for the change; there were advantages to attending town school; Edward would meet more kids his own age and have more opportunities. But his aunt said the best education in the world took place in one-room country schools.

One of the kids in Edward's class complained she had to go to town school because of Frances. But his teacher said that wasn't true. The schools were not closing because of Frances; it was because it was the way of the world. Edward believed his teacher. All the country schools in the whole state surely would not close just because of Frances.

* * * * *

Frances shouldn't have tried to cross that creek; she should have taken the long way home, been more careful. But what did she know? She was just a kid; she was too brave. Before his sister drowned, I didn't know Edward, but on that last country school afternoon, I sat across the aisle from him. I was one of the "town students" who sang in the Turner County School chorus that day. I remember Frances from track meets. She got a lot of ribbons—blue ones, red ones, never yellow ones for third place. Everyone now knew who Edward was; he was the brother who had been with Frances when she drowned; he was the only one who could have saved her.

We were more than a hundred kids sitting on the bleachers that day, singing in the final Turner County School chorus. Every once in a while, I would take a look at Edward across the aisle. He was always staring straight ahead with no expression on his face.

At the end of the program, Miss Hemphill, the county school superintendent, a tiny dark-haired woman, powerful as a freight train, came to the microphone. "This is the last time that all the Turner Country Schools will all be together," she said, craning her neck upward. She hesitated, her voice seemed to waver. "We will dedicate our final number to Frances Petersen. We will all sing 'I Walked Today Where Jesus Walked.' Please rise."

I glanced at Edward, who looked straight ahead at the stage where Miss Hemphill, Mrs. Burns, and the other teachers stood in a row between three flags—the United States, South Dakota, and another one I didn't recognize.

A pianist played an introduction, and we began to sing:

"I walked today where Jesus walked in days of long ago…"

It seemed a strange song to sing. Jesus had walked on the other side of the world, never on the Petersen's creek. I felt awfully sad singing that song, and when I looked up, I saw that I wasn't the only one. Miss Hemphill, the principal, was crying! Miss Hemphill, who was in charge of everything in all the schools, was weeping! Whether she was weeping for Frances or because the country schools were closing, I didn't know.

"I wept today where Jesus wept in days of long ago…"

I looked across the aisle at Edward and saw tears were now running down his cheeks. He made no effort to stop them, probably so he wouldn't be noticed. His face had a hungry look, and in spite of biting my lip, I started crying too. Frances was just a kid like the rest of us. Now things would never be the same, not for any of us.

*****

Now, many years later, I too have known the hunger I first saw in Edward's face that day when we sang, "I Walked Today Where Jesus Walked" in memory of Frances. It is the hunger for self-forgiveness, the pain of regret where there is no recompense, no going back to the way things could have been, no possibility of changes that could result in things turning out differently.

Without forgiveness, life becomes entangled in a Gordian knot of regret and resentment; with forgiveness, we learn to be merciful to ourselves as well as others. Frances is best remembered by enjoying life, being courageous, avoiding thin ice, and sometimes even turning back.

5

Willis

In the hospital:

Voices…voices…can't speak…can't move…m*ust be…dying.*

Fred…Lars…Jens…my brothers, help with the wheat…harvest.

"No. No more medicine. Pain…something for the pain."

Need some help. Not much time. And Ida…dearest Ida…I have missed you.

"Harald. Why are you here? Go home. Your family."

Fred. Start that side…The field is large…time so short. So tired…sun…is shining.

"What did you say? Laura. Ida. Elsie. My son… All of you here. Who? Not her. Don't want to see her… No…I need to go…need to help with the harvest."

Darker. Much darker…hardly see the field…Glad Fred is here to help. I suppose Ida is worried…Storm is coming…feel the wind…it goes through the fields like a giant thresher…the light…a bright light…so much left in the fields…

"I give…thanks…for…my life."

Look at the sun against the storm clouds, Fred. Ida. Father…Mother…glad to see you. Glad to be…in the fields again…need the rain…The wheat is waving.

"Good…bye."

That evening, Willis Ibsen died.

* * * * *

Only a few months prior, Uncle Will and his wife, Aunt Lucy, had visited us in the small town where we lived in South Dakota, not far from where the Ibsen brothers had originally homesteaded.

Uncle Will began his day with a shot of whiskey, pouring a shot of Jack Daniels from a bottle he stored in our refrigerator. Because I was in the kitchen the first afternoon after he arrived, I saw Uncle Will, after rising from his nap, open up our refrigerator, and down a shot of whiskey. Realizing something was amiss, I reported him to my mother. She came into the kitchen right away.

"Will," my mother said "It's three o'clock in the afternoon!"

"It is?" Will was embarrassed. "Oh my gracious! I thought it was morning!"

Their visit that year brought even more embarrassment but to us rather than to Uncle Will. Like most people in the 1950s, we had only one bathroom in our house, and it was very busy on school mornings.

I was first in the bathroom the next morning when my older brother David knocked impatiently at the door. He wanted, then needed to come in. I continued to brush my teeth. It seemed only a few minutes later when David returned, and this time he pounded on the door. "Hurry up!" he said.

"I'll be out in a minute!" I called to him as I proceeded to brush my hair.

"You better be!" he said and went away again. I hurriedly combed my bangs, then opened the door just as Aunt Lucy came shuffling down from upstairs with her giant makeup kit and walked past me right into the bathroom.

Oh dear, I thought. *Now he'll really be mad.* I sat down on the stairs facing the bathroom door just as my brother came marching angrily from the dining room. Seeing the bathroom door closed and not seeing me, he pounded on the door with his fist. "Get out of there, you hag! You could spend the whole day in there combing your hair and it wouldn't do a bit of good!"

My brother turned and saw me sitting on the steps putting on my socks. "Who is in the bathroom?" he managed.

"Aunt Lucy."

He groaned just as Aunt Lucy came rushing out looking like she was running away from a robbery, and David got into the bathroom.

No amount of apologizing, primarily from us or my mother, would satisfy Aunt Lucy. She was upset. That wasn't the end of it.

To make matters worse, the next night at dinner, my father was telling all of us about a very old woman he had visited who had thirty-seven children whom she had taken care of after the civil war.

Aunt Lucy asked, "All her own?"

"No," my father said. "They were mostly orphans."

But I already had been struck with unstoppable giggles and was laughing at the prospect of having thirty-seven children, but trying not to, making it worse. Unfortunately, the giggles got so bad that my dad caught them, and in spite of himself, he started laughing too, which made my brother laugh. Uncle Will's shoulders were shaking with laughter. My mother managed to keep her decorum, but then my sister asked, "What's so funny?" which made me, my dad, brother, and Will all start laughing again.

Mother tried to explain to Aunt Lucy that we were sorry, we didn't mean to be rude. It was just a matter of my giggle attacks. Again we apologized, but Aunt Lucy was furious. When they left, Aunt Lucy gave my sister Karma a whole dollar bill and walked right past my brother and me. But we each got a silver dollar from Uncle Will.

* * * * *

The long distance phone call was unexpected. Uncle Will had suffered a major stroke. He would probably not "make it." Aunt Lucy had found him in the bathroom on the floor in the middle of the night. She said she did not have the strength to move him, and so she decided to leave him there until morning before calling the ambulance.

"How could she leave him like that? What's the matter with her?" my mother asked.

Obviously, there was no good answer. Late in his life, years after his wife died, Will had married Lucy, his younger brother's widow. It was not a happy marriage. Will's last years were difficult, but a divorce was not a consideration in those days; divorce indicated a failure of commitment. Will would manage, and manage well he did, until he lay dying in the hospital, sedated, no longer able to control his feelings. He did not want his wife in the hospital room.

Immediately upon hearing the news of Will's hospitalization, my father flew to Colorado Springs in spite of our family's limited finances. We stood in awe as my father boarded the airplane. To fly in an airplane!

Handsome and wise, Will was one of three Ibsen brothers—Lars, Will, and Janus, who first joined their father, Mads, in Viborg in March, 1890. Uncle Will lived his adult life in South Dakota, Montana, and Colorado. He was my surrogate paternal grandfather. Lars, my grandfather, died from tuberculosis when my father was a young child.

Barely in his teens, Will helped his father and brothers build railroad tracks, only to come up empty handed (twice) at the end of a month's hard labor because the railroad companies had gone broke. Finally, they were forced to live in a cave built into a hillside; their younger sister Ingeborg came to help cook and keep the cave neat and clean.

Eventually, after laboring for years, the men were able to bring the remaining children and finally their mother to America.

Will enjoyed ranching with his brother Fred and later owned a successful International Harvester farm implement dealership in Montana. Along the way, Will married Ida and nurtured the development and marriages of five children, tending carefully to the trials and successes of his businesses as well his children's lives. When we were growing up, Fred and Will and their children took an interest in our family, because of their commitment to their brother Lars. We saw Will the most—Uncle Will, as we always called him. He had a western twinkle in his clear blue eyes, and when he visited, he always brought silver dollars and gave them to each of us children—silver dollars, which matched his silver hair. To this day, I always think of Will every first day of spring, his birthday, a day full of the promise of green grass and a coming summer of unrestrained fun.

The spring I was twelve years old, the Ibsen family gathered in Colorado Springs for Uncle Will's eightieth birthday. Will's eyes twinkled like snow-flakes on a bright winter day. His face crinkled with laughter as he smoked his pipe. Will enjoyed his eightieth birthday surrounded by family—children, grandchildren, nephews, nieces, their children, and his brother, Fred. Some lucky daughters, nieces, or nephews were able to talk privately with Will, the patriarch, asking his counsel, which always came as solid and plain as a dead bolt lock.

After the festivities and before we left Colorado Springs following that last birthday gathering, I walked with my father and great uncle outside their home toward a pond on the other side of the park. It was to be their last talk and walk. Halfway across, we stopped to look back at Will's home nestled before the background of Pikes Peak. It was a clear summer day.

"You have a beautiful home here, Will," my father said.

Uncle Will paused a moment. "It doesn't mean anything to me," he said, emotionless, stating a simple fact. It was as if to say, *"Don't be misled. This is not what life is about."*

My father simply nodded. It was not my father's way to make things seem better than they were; things are as they are! The three of us continued our walk across the park.

* * * * *

Uncle Will's funeral was held in Viborg, South Dakota, only a few miles from where he had once lived in a cave with his father and brothers. My father, as minister, spoke with uncharacteristic emotion, thanking God for all that Uncle Will and his generation had given. His voice cracked as he said, "I wonder what we have given our children, the next generation. I fear it is not nearly as much as was given us."

I wanted to say, "No, Dad. Don't worry! You have given us a lot!" I had a sense of Ibsens, Juhls, and Rodholms going back to the time people began, doing the best they could for their families—and we kids moving forward, uncertainly, to an unknown future.

Now I am filled with gratitude for what my parents, grandparents, and many others have given me, and I wonder, *What have I given my children, the next generation? Is it adequate?* Confronted by mounting complexities as society "advances," and my own limitations, I know I have not done nearly enough. But I also know our children and the future are amazing.

The three oldest Ibsen brothers, Willis, Lars, and Janus. In 1899, Lars won the National Fair prize for the best butter in South Dakota (56 state creameries and several European countries participated). Will succeeded Lars, who became ill, and won the first prize for South Dakota in 1900; Janus won first prize four more times.

6

Borge

Think! Think! Think! Think! Think!

Five diamond-shaped signs with blood-red and death-black lettering against a white background, scream a demand for attention to one's mortality on the corner of South Dakota State Highway 19, where the flat, seemingly irrevocably straight pavement suddenly bends ninety degrees north, the only corner for miles: **Five people died on this corner! Think! Slow down! Or you will crash and die!**

South Dakota highways are decorated with these fateful signs; each diamond-painted piece of metal notifies drivers and passengers of the precise places where traffic fatalities have occurred. The number of people who died in traffic accidents at the location is simply a matter of counting the signs.

In the fifties, South Dakota implemented its first speed limit. Up until then, life was relatively simple; in addition to the lack of speed limits, there were only two psychiatrists in the entire state.

Perhaps there was no relationship between no speed limit and few psychiatrists except that self-reliance and self-monitoring were desirable and even necessary qualities for living well in South Dakota.

Following my sixteenth birthday, my father accompanied me to the town of Parker, the Turner County seat, to get my first driver's license.

"You have a birth certificate?" the man asked from behind the counter in the old courthouse, where rites of passage, such as licenses to drive, marry, or proof of death, were handed out like *Good Housekeeping* seals of approval. "Here," I said, and handed him the strange piece of paper proving my birth date.

My father stood behind me. He still seemed slightly rattled. At the beginning of our journey to Parker, he had let me drive our Chevrolet Impala. Backing out, I had hit the only tree anywhere near the driveway, denting the back fender and shattering his usual calm demeanor. "What are you doing?" he had shouted, a question requiring no answer.

Gratefully, Dad drove the rest of the way to the courthouse. Fortunately for me, in those days, a person did not need to be able to drive at all, let alone drive well, to get a driver's license. I only had to go to the courthouse, prove I was at least sixteen, and pay the fee. My brother knew of one man who was so feeble they brought his license out to him in his Model A.

"That will be fifty cents," the clerk said to me. I already had two quarters waiting, an hour's wages from working in the local grocery store.

"Here you are," he said, handing me my precious license. Only one hour's pay had purchased my rights to adulthood. I was ecstatic and looked at my new official license with adolescent awe. Now I *could* drive if, of course, I could *drive*, and that would be achieved with practice. Ever since birth, I have experienced difficulty with machinery. Almost every machine I encounter dislikes me at first, and expresses its disapproval in unpleasant ways. I was trying not to take the car's behavior personally and held firm to my belief that sooner or later, that car and I would learn to get along. Sooner or later.

Nevertheless, I had to agree that hitting the tree was a problem. I simply had no idea that when I stepped on the gas pedal, the car would shoot out of the driveway like it did, and to make matters worse, that I would confuse the accelerator for the brake. Before I knew it, we had smashed into the tree; without seat belts, we were quite shaken.

"I'm driving!" my father had said when I hit the tree, and he nearly leaped out of the car.

"Okay," I said. Actually, I was glad, having lost what little confidence I had. My dad seemed nervous. The important thing was that I was going to get my license.

"You have to *think* about what you're doing," my father explained. I knew that. Hitting the tree was behind me; that was just a bad beginning. After all, now I had my treasured license. The day was sunny and beautiful.

"Do you want to drive?" he asked gently when we returned to the car, but he spoke without much enthusiasm.

"No, that's all right," I said. I had my license, the first step. Someday I would learn how to drive. Everyone learns to drive except a few old ladies. Learning to drive was like learning to walk or go to the bathroom. I had not thought a little boy whom I babysat would ever learn to go to the bathroom, but he did. If Kevin could learn to go to the bathroom, I could learn to drive.

Dad gladly took the wheel.

* * * * *

A few weeks later, there was a terrible accident. A '52 Ford with five men inside was traveling at a very high rate of speed. Their car went off Highway 19 south of the town of Viborg at two o'clock in the morning. They missed the highway's only curve. The Ford overturned, and all of them were killed. One of them was a brother of a man in the congregation where my father was the minister. Soon five diamond-shaped signs, each with the word "THINK!" on them, would be erected on the fatal corner.

How could they have missed that corner? They all knew the road, and it was the only corner for miles. Yes, they had been drinking, but they should have known to turn. It was the only thing they had to think about. But I had hit the tree, the only tree near the driveway. How could I have hit the tree?

Everyone in town talked about the accident.

"Too bad. He was going back to Denmark to see his mother."

"Now he'll never get there."

"I didn't know him very well."

"No one knew him very well,

"It is too bad he never learned English well. It held him back."

"He got in with the wrong crowd."

"I feel bad for the brother."

"And his family back home!"

"Such a young man."

"He should have known better."

"Liquor will do that to you."

"Never ride with a drunk driver, that's for sure."

"He was an excellent painter."

"Borge painted our house. He did a wonderful job. Cleaned up after himself too."

"They must have been going eighty miles an hour."

"I wonder if they will have an open casket?"

I had not listened to the answer to the last question, and later wished I had paid attention. Late in the morning of Borge's funeral, scheduled for later that afternoon, I went to practice my lesson on the church's organ. I was taking lessons on the Hammond organ and having similar mechanical difficulties as I did with cars; sometimes I hit the volume pedal as if it were an accelerator.

Opening the doorway to the church that morning, I was aware of that peculiar holy smell that lingered in the church, as if the hymns that had been sung almost a week ago had a fragrance. I walked across the floorboards; they creaked from my own footsteps, disturbing the quiet of the empty sanctuary, then resounded on the window sills which crackled a response. I loved the way the light came through the colored glass rectangles on the perimeters of the frosty church windows. No stained glass art figures in this prairie church; the sun shone through the small gold-, blue-, and crimson-colored glass surrounding translucent glass panes, making patches of blue, cherry and amber colors on the carpet leading to the altar.

Above the wood-carved altar was a large painting of Jesus helping a lost sheep. Danish words in gold letters underneath the altar offered an explanation of what was happening. Jesus was climbing down to rescue the sheep that had fallen into a ravine, a steep embankment. The sheep was looking up, frightened and grateful, at Jesus, who had left the other sheep to fend for themselves, which seemed a bit risky. A halo shone around Jesus's head. Apparently the sheep sensed this was someone who could be trusted. But then Jesus was the only chance the sheep had; the ravine was very steep, and that sheep couldn't get out by himself. At least, *someone* was coming to help him.

I was looking and thinking about all this as I walked up the aisle, but then I stopped in my tracks on the sunlit pattern of amber-colored carpet.

Directly in front of the altar stretched out in his coffin was…Borge! The undertaker had brought Borge's body to the church and placed his casket in front of the altar for visitation prior to the funeral.

Instead of his white paint clothes, Borge was dressed up in a suit. Awful folds of white satin surrounded his face.

Oh my god! Borge. A dead man! I panicked, turned, and ran out of the church as quickly as I could. I ran next door to the parsonage where I lived and quickly opened the screen door. No one was home. I ran up the stairs to my bedroom and sat down on the bed on the blue-and-white quilt my grandmother had made. I sat there shaking and clutching my music books for a long time. I could see Borge's ashen face, his eyes closed. Very, very dead.

I hardly knew him; I had no idea what Borge was really like. But now he was dead. He was really dead.

Think! Think! Think! Think! Think!

*＊＊＊＊

For years after Borge's life-ending, utterly lacking in confidence, I was unable to drive an automobile, no matter who tried to teach me. Whenever I took the wheel, when meeting a car on the highway, I would realize I was within inches of killing someone, perhaps myself—a mere two feet from Borge's fate.

What would it be like, lying in a casket in front of the altar, unable to move, unable to think or feel?

Because of my fear and inherent incompatibility with machinery, I didn't learn to drive for another eleven years. During that time, I renewed my driver's license in three states—Indiana, Illinois, and finally a provisional license in Iowa. Still I couldn't drive. Finally, at age 27, far from public transportation, with a baby and a toddler and a husband frequently unavailable to drive us anywhere, out of desperation, I learned to drive.

"Just keep it between the curbs, lady," my instructor told me soothingly. "Just keep it between the curbs."

And finally, I did.

* * * * *

As a teenager, I first confronted my own life-ending when confronting Borge in the casket. I kept thinking, *What would it be like to die in an automobile crash? What would it be like to be dead?* In response to the "THINK" signs—with their fearsome black and blood-red lettering—I "over-thunk" and as a result, was unable to learn to drive for quite a long while.

Curiously, I now love to drive, and I believe I am a very good driver. As for life, I have taken several detours from my path, but sooner or later, like everyone else, I return to my path and live as much in the present as possible.

Instead of "Think! Think! Think!" The signs in South Dakota should command "Live! Live! Live!"

And what about Borge?

Borge went on to another state of being, where there are no "Think!" signs and where there is no time. Borge continues on his path beyond time and thought.

PART II

Asking Why

7

Andy

Albert Thompson. Alan Thompson...More
than twenty Thompson names were listed on the
white pages of the Sioux Falls telephone book but
no "Andrew Thompson." What was Andy's father's
name? I had no way of knowing. Again, I searched
my purse, looking for Andy's telephone number, but
it hadn't materialized in the two minutes since I had
looked for it before. Again, I checked my billfold,
which was silly because I had checked in all these
places several times and been unable to find the
scrap of yellow-lined paper where I had scribbled the
phone number. What had I done with it?

In only a few weeks, I was scheduled to attend
the Ashram, a conference of college students in the
Colorado Rockies. I had planned to ride from my
home in South Dakota with a group of Augustana
college students from Sioux Falls, whom I did not
know. I was to confirm our tentative agreement to
ride with them. If I didn't find the phone number,

I wouldn't be going. I decided just to start calling Thompsons and chose "Albert."

"Hello," I said. "I'm looking for an Andy Thompson who goes to Augustana College. Is this the right number?"

"No, it isn't," an annoyed man's voice answered.

"I'm very sorry," I said. "Goodbye."

But the person had already hung up and I was embarrassed. *Forget it*, I thought. *Forget it.* After all, I did have an alternative. I could contact some college friends who were coming from Des Moines, Iowa. Someone would need to drive me to a meeting location somewhere in Nebraska. Well, if I wanted to go…

I explained the problem to my father that evening, and he agreed to drive me to Omaha. "Thanks, Dad," I said, grateful that he didn't bother with a lecture.

* * * * *

On a beautiful early summer day a couple of months later, my father and I made the trip to the rendezvous, a restaurant on Highway 6 on the outskirts of Omaha. Scott and Katherine were already there, waiting patiently in front of the café. I hurriedly grabbed my suitcase out of the car, not wanting to keep them waiting. When I looked at my dad, I felt more vulnerable than when I left for college. We made our goodbyes quickly. Scott started his car, and I waved to my dad as we drove off; he waved back.

Katherine had the front seat, but I had the whole back seat, a welcome luxury. If I had gone with Andy, I would have shared the back seat with two other kids. When I had spoken to him on the phone, Andy had assured me that there was room for me, but I had wondered if it wouldn't be crowded—there would be five of us.

The Nebraska landscape whizzing by seemed inordinately repetitious—farmers plowing their fields, acres of dazzling wheat growing in the sun, hundreds of cattle grazing. Scott slowed down only for some of the Nebraska towns we drove through.

"Is there a beaver crossing Nebraska?" I asked, even though I realized it was a family joke (there is a town named Beaver Crossing). Most family jokes are clever only to those who learned them when they were four years old. Neither Scott nor Katherine were amused, and didn't say anything when we finally drove through Beaver Crossing.

Every moment, every mile, took us closer to the Colorado mountains. Occasionally we chatted, catching up with news of the few people we all knew, sharing expectations for the conference we were attending, relating stories from our summer jobs, plans for the next school year. After a while, I fell asleep.

Waking, I heard Scott talking to Katherine: "Listen, listen to this." He turned up the sound of the news on the radio:

> The students, whose names are
> being withheld pending notification
> of relatives, were on their way
> to Colorado. The driver of the
> semitruck, who survived, is being
> held for failure to yield the right of
> way.

"What? What did they say?" I asked, barely awake.

"Some students were killed. They were from South Dakota."

"From South Dakota? From Sioux Falls?"

"They didn't say. Names have not yet been released."

"That was my ride! I was going to ride with them. Are you sure?"

"Well, there was an accident."

"What did they say? What exactly did they say?"

Katherine looked at me. "Just four South Dakota students were killed, collided with some semi."

"I think it was on Highway 30," Scott said.

"That was my ride. I know it was."

"Did you know them?" Scott asked. He had slowed down.

"No, I only talked to Andy once. I lost his phone number."

"You lost his phone number?"

"Yes, that's why I called you."

"Do you want me to stop?"

"No, it's okay. I'll be all right." But it wasn't all right. I felt like I had just heard news about my own life ending…over the radio.

Katharine looked at me. "Maybe…maybe you were meant to come with us."

"I don't think so!" I said.

Katherine looked at me, puzzled. "Seriously, maybe you were meant to live."

And what about them, I wondered, but didn't say anything. I wished I were not headed for a religious conference. *And what about that semi driver?* It sounded like it was his fault, and he was alive.

We rode in silence for a while, waiting for the next newscast, which didn't provide much more information, but confirmed that all four students from Sioux Falls had been killed in an automobile crash. The three of us didn't talk much after that. I couldn't help but imagine what would have happened if I had been in that car—how my family and friends would have reacted to my life-ending. I should have cleaned up my room and gotten rid of my diary before going on this trip. I thought about the four kids with whom I was to have shared this ride and now would never meet. I didn't even know what they looked like. It occurred to me that if I had gone with them, they might not have died. The timing would have been different; the car would have been in a different place and not been hit by that semi.

Hours and hours later, we drove into the YMCA resort in the Rocky Mountains. Enormous mountains with snow-covered toppings stretched majestically around the camp as if to shelter and protect it from the rest of the world.

Quickly, we got out of the car and stretched our legs. Scott let out a yell, "Yeoooow!" like a giddy cowboy celebrating the end of a difficult round-up. The trip had been long, and the last half of it had been gloomy.

I looked around at all the splendor of the mountains fading in the sunset and felt better.

"Isn't this gorgeous?" Katherine said quietly.

I nodded. "Yes," I said, almost whispering. "I'm glad to be here." I meant it!

* * * * *

The Ashram was a retreat, a place for spiritual renewal, but the tragedy of the students' life-endings hung over us like dark velvet drapes shutting out light on a bright summer day.

Students from throughout the country gathered in the chapel for our first evening service. A clergyman announced the deaths of the students for those few who had not heard about the accident. He asked us to pray for Andy, Carey, Lou, Janice, and their families. Heads bowed around me in prayer. A few kids wept. It was difficult, strange.

What good would prayer do? I thought. *They were dead. How could we help them now?* They were gone. They wouldn't be coming to the Ashram; they wouldn't be going back to college, to their friends, to their families.

My escape from fate had bizarre consequences as word spread throughout the camp. "She was to have been with them, but lost their phone number and had to find another ride. How about that?" The notoriety made me uncomfortable. A question haunted me—was there meaning in their deaths? Did God plan for Andy and the others to be killed? Surely I had not escaped death because I was disorganized.

It was also disturbing that our grieving time was so short. How quickly their names were forgotten. It could have been I who was so easily forgotten. What difference did our lives make, anyway? Except for prayers during services, the accident was rarely talked about after the first night. We were young and had come to have a good time. No one in the camp personally knew the students who had been killed. For both religious and practical reasons, the directors of the Ashram didn't want to dwell on the tragedy. This I understood, but nevertheless it troubled me that we were so quickly forgetting them and going on with our lives, which, of course, was what we must do. Andy and the others had died trying to get to the Ashram, but after they died, we closed the gaping hole they had left in the universe, as if they didn't matter. Didn't we owe them something?

I captured the attention of Dave, a well-built divinity student from Pacific Lutheran, and fell somewhat in love, a sweet one-week uncomplicated, precious conference romance. He was attracted to my questioning ways; I admired his dark curls, muscular arms, and calm take-care-of-others demeanor. By the second day we sat together at all our meals, attended as many of the same sessions as possible, took walks together along mountain paths holding hands, and by the end of the week, we would, at last, kiss.

"Are you really going to become a minister?" I asked on our second walk together.

"I really am."

"I can't pray anymore," I said. I thought I should let him know. "I don't have any…any concept of who or what God is. How can I pray? Praying seems like talking to myself. If I had some concept of God, it would help."

Dave was sympathetic, but he never tried to answer my questions. "Don't worry about it. You have a right to question. The answers will come. You'll see."

The next day, I brought up my dilemma to my favorite discussion group. Sitting outside on the lawn surrounded by the Rocky Mountains, I took a sudden departure from our topic, which had something to do with Jeremiah. Everyone but me seemed to have their beliefs intact; it was late in the week for expressions of doubt, but I was running out of time. "I don't have a concept of God," I said. "I don't believe in a super-guy-in-the-sky God anymore, a God who keeps track of everything we do, who gives and takes things from us, who answers prayers or not. I don't know what it means to believe in God. Not anymore."

Some of the students stared at me, or looked down, but Margo, the discussion leader, a tall, pleasant woman with a puckish haircut, said "Maybe God isn't a concept. Maybe God is a complex."

That changed something in my head, a shift from whom to what God was—a complex. I thought about that. Perhaps God was a complex of interconnected parts, but what made up the complex?

On the last night of the Ashram, Dave and I took our final walk together. He was returning to the Northwest, I to the Midwest. We had no future, only a precious, sweet, no-pressure present.

I looked up at him, enjoying his strength. "I love the mountains. *They* are real."

"I will lift mine eyes unto the hills," he murmured.

"Oh boy, you really are going to be a minister."

"From whence cometh my help," he continued, doggedly reciting the Psalm but now in a whisper. "My help cometh from the Lord, who made heaven and earth."

"I wish I could take that mountain back home with me."

"You can. You can take it home."

"How can I do that?"

"You have a heck of an imagination."

I smiled. "Okay. Yes, I can do that. I will take... *that* mountain home with me and put it in my backyard. No, I'll put it in the middle of the college campus."

"Then do it," he said. "Take it with you."

"Okay," I said. "I will."

And then we kissed for the first and last time.

* * * * *

I took the image of the mountain home with me and put it on the Grand View College campus. Occasionally, I would "lift my eyes unto the hills," the imaginary mountain, and for quite a few weeks, it helped. Then, the mountain began to fade away a little more each week, until I forgot about it entirely. Dave and I never wrote to each other.

But the answer Margo had given stuck with me. God was not some super being up there. God was a complex. It wasn't much of an answer, but it made sense; I could pray again. Margo had helped reframe the question—a complex. What made up that complex became the new question.

God sees the sparrow fall, but that doesn't mean he rescues it or places a net underneath, not always. Nor do I believe God pushes sparrows off tree branches when they aren't ready to fly. What I wasn't ready to accept was a fellow sparrow deliberately leaping to its own destruction.

8

Herb

After two years at Grand View College, then a two-year school where I had basked in the Grundtvigian Danish tradition, it was time to choose a college to complete my education. Shimer College—the poster on the bulletin board in Old Main intrigued me. Shimer's curriculum was comprised of a purist form of Robert Maynard Hutchins's philosophy of education—all discussion classes, all original readings. This Great Books Education sounded fascinating, but my initial response was that it was also unrealistic. (Later, I learned that Hutchins had studied Grundtvig, who has been a connection throughout my life.) Nevertheless, I met with their college representative, who offered me a trip to Mount Carroll, Illinois, where the college was then located, only a few miles from my grandparents' home in Clinton, Iowa. I decided to visit the campus, visit my grandparents, and take a look at this very unusual school.

Strangely enough, the Shimer College class I visited on a Saturday morning was Nat Sci I; it was all about physics, of no interest to me, or so I thought, but when I sat in on the round table of discussion, I couldn't help but become fascinated. I wanted to have read the material and was tempted to join in the discussion, even uninformed. It was also the day I heard the name of John Mitchell Martin, a "talented student poet." I instantly felt a connection with this person whom I had not met. When offered a full tuition scholarship and a job in the cafeteria, Shimer became the college of my choice.

When I arrived on campus at Shimer, I knew who I was and what I was about. When I left Shimer College, I had only the vaguest notion.

My job as a waitress included serving formal dinners one night a week and Sunday noon. On the first such event, while carrying a huge tray of fresh blueberry pies, I came through the swinging doors of the dining room just as a waiter came hell bent from the other direction. (I learned later that he was in a race with another waiter to see who could finish their tables first.) A multi-tympanic-resounding crash! Both trays flew up, and the two of us landed on the floor, our bodies decorated with blueberry pie and surrounded by cascades of broken dishes. As was customary whenever the sound of dish-breaking occurred in the dining room, the students broke into applause. I stood up and made an elaborate curtsy while my coworker scraped pie off his shirt and pants.

The food manager asked me to come to his office the next morning after breakfast. Having broken so many dishes my first night at a formal dinner, I expected at least a reprimand and maybe even being fired. Instead I was promoted to the job of noon hostess and given a raise of five cents an hour. Incompetence rewarded! While a boost to $1.65 an hour was not a great pay raise, becoming a hostess was a promotion. My new tasks included welcoming guests, serving as cashier for visitors, and making sure the students wore shoes, an issue in the sixties.

When I emerged from the manager's office, I was greeted by Herb, a fellow worker, who was washing pots and pans. Herb was one of only a few black students among the college's 225 "community of scholars."

"So what happened?" he asked.

I told him about my promotion.

"Congratulations," he said.

"I thought I was going to get fired."

"I think your curtsy did the trick." Herb grinned. "You'll be a good hostess."

"I'm a lousy waitress. I know that."

He smiled; I noticed he didn't disagree.

* * * * *

Shimer College had a wonderful food service in those days. I never ate better in my life than the two years I spent at that college. Formal dinners at Shimer College were nothing less than gourmet affairs.

Historically, the college had been a finishing school for young ladies, then became an experimental college of the University of Chicago before becoming an independent college, which for a time was loosely associated with the Episcopal Church. These contrasting and sometimes contradictory elements showed through the college's personality like fascinating undergarments. On Wednesday nights and Sunday noons, Shimer reverted to the finishing school style of formal Victorian dining. The rest of the week most students wore antiestablishment clothing, primarily torn jeans and holey shirts. Dressing well during the school day seemed to suggest intellectual failure and errant materialism.

Herb was one of Shimer's many contradictions. Tall, black, athletic and handsome, he fit in perfectly with a white, nonathletic, somewhat nerdy student body. During my first semester, he successfully lobbied the college administration into offering a new course, Irrational Man. Adding a new course to Shimer's "canonical" curriculum was not an easy task. (Textbooks were not allowed on campus, and reading five to seven books a week was not unusual.) Herb had recruited me, perhaps thinking I would agree that life was not rational. He insisted, and I concurred, that Shimer needed a new elective course, an antidote to the required killer-course for all seniors—Organization, Methods and Principles of Philosophy—with its heavy emphasis on Hegel, Kant, and Oppenheimer.

"We're going to have this great course," Herb had said, cornering me in the cafeteria. "But we need at least eight people to sign up for it. It's going to be fantastic. The faculty—Miller, Weiser, and Olson—will team-teach it along with several others. Will you sign up for it?"

Eventually I agreed, due to Herb's constant pleading, and because it sounded great. Irrational Man turned out to be one of the best classes I ever had. We read, listened, discussed the existentialists, soaked ourselves in modern art, and wrote creative autobiographies in the form of poems and paintings. In one semester, I wrote a very long poem and read seven books by Søren Kierkegaard.

I did well scholastically at Shimer as I entered my senior year, in spite of the fact that I had secretly fallen in love and was a nervous wreck about what to do about it. I was in love with a man who was married, yes, the poet. There was no way I was going to have an affair with John Martin, even though a friend of his pleaded with me to do so and "get it over with!" As a result of the strain, John left the campus the semester prior to his graduation and was in the process of getting a divorce. Even though there had been no affair, I felt responsible. I was confused and overwhelmed, and no longer had a simple definition of who I was. Still, I clung desperately to the notion that the answers to life's questions would become clear if I remained true to myself. But who was I? Surely, not someone to become involved with a married man.

Working in the cafeteria had become a welcome activity where life was simple. All I needed to do or be was the cafeteria hostess.

Herb's job had also changed. Now he mopped the floor in the evening. Often Herb would mop late at night, always whistling. He had a fabulous whistle. At night I would hear him cross the campus quadrangle as he headed for the men's dorm, whistling a strange melody that resounded through the night.

Finally, on December 19th, the very special night of our Christmas dinner, I was beginning to relax. Exams were nearly over. I was eager to go home, be with my family, celebrate Christmas in Nebraska, think things over. All that remained before I left on the Union Pacific from Savannah was a fabulous Christmas dinner and a Nat Sci exam the next day.

The dining room was beautifully dressed with boughs of Christmas greens and red ribbons. White tablecloths and candlelight glimmered throughout the dining room. What a shock to realize that wrinkled suits, strange-patterned neckties, skirts, and high heels could transform even the most reluctant scholars into fashion kings and queens. Only a few holdouts declined to set foot in the dining room for a "dress dinner" no matter how tempted they were by roast turkey, sirloin, ham, potatoes, cranberries, several vegetables, salads, and chocolate mousse.

The table grace, an Anglican version, echoed through the hall from the college president, and our Christmas dinner began.

"Where's Herb?" I asked, looking across the lighted candles at the empty place setting at our table for ten.

"I don't know. He'll be coming. We're saving him a place."

"Herb would get dressed up for a dinner like this," freckle-faced Rosie said. It was the first, perhaps only time, I ever saw her in a skirt.

"Should someone try to call him?" Alicia, who was the evening's table hostess, asked.

No one moved. There were only a few phones in the dorms; to make a call meant leaving dinner and locating a telephone. Herb probably would not hear it anyway.

"I doubt he forgot. Maybe he fell asleep."

Alicia began serving in the formal style, dishing the food for each person beginning on her far left, serving the "ladies" first, clockwise, one by one according to their preferences ("no gravy," "a little more meat, please") and then serving the "gentlemen." Across the white tablecloths and flickering candlelight, we all waited patiently until everyone was served, as we chatted about the amazing transformations of our schoolmates throughout the room. Sam had shaved! Would the world end?

Time quickly passed while we ate heartedly, thoroughly enjoying our delicious dinner and the festive spirit. Before we knew it, we were eating dessert, the famed elegant chocolate mousse. Still no Herb.

It was time to leave.

"He'll be sorry to have missed *this* dinner."
Rosie said.

And she is sorry to have missed him, I thought.

Before I left the dining room, I dawdled for a
few minutes in the entry hoping to compare notes
on the Nat Sci exam tomorrow. Slowly, I became
aware of a strange buzzing among the students in
tones which sounded almost like a Gregorian chant.
I looked around me. I heard a girl crying; students
were mysteriously gathered in corners. Most faces
were stark with no expression, but some had looks
of horror. What had happened? Perhaps there was
something on the news? I heard phrases.

"Oh my god!"

"His roommate found him."

"Jesus, Mary, and Joseph!"

"What the hell for, that's what I want to know!"

"I heard he blew his head right off."

I turned to Alexander, a freshman student
standing next to me. "What happened?"

He stared at me blankly. "It's Herb Taylor."

"What about Herb?

"He shot himself."

"He what?"

"He's dead."

"You're kidding."

Alexander shook his head; again I heard crying
in the background. A look of guilt mixed with excitement, fear, and pain marred Alex's face. "The police
are all there now. They've got the dorm roped off."

Through the window across from the annex, I saw shadows moving in front of McNeil Hall—then a police car, an ambulance with circling globes of light.

"They say it is a real mess."

My body went weak. Turning from Alexander, I made my way over to one of the windows that looked out on the quadrangle. I placed my head against a cold window pane and held on to the sill for support.

"Easy…easy. Just take it easy." A man's hand was on my shoulder. I turned my head slightly and saw the hand belonged to Mr. Armstrong, my Shakespeare professor. I continued to stare out the window. His touch on my shoulder released a wounded sob from deep inside me. Shivers collided inside my body.

"He shouldn't have done it." I said.

"I know."

In the background, several people were weeping, but I also heard someone laughing.

"Are you all right?" he asked.

I nodded and pressed my forehead on the cold December window. "Why did he do it?" I asked. Mr. Armstrong taught Shakespeare.

He should know if anyone could.

"We'll never know."

"It's Christmas," I said. An inane protest, but it was Christmas, for God's sake!

Mr. Armstrong gave me a final pat on the shoulder. "You all right now?"

The chills were less violent, but I felt dizzy. I leaned more heavily toward the comfort of the cold window and nodded.

Mr. Armstrong withdrew and left to check on another student. I turned and made my way through the after-dinner crowd noticing that fellow students now looked unfamiliar; I hardly recognized them. Someone called my name, but I kept walking. I did not want to talk to anyone. Herb, someone I knew so well, had done something he could not possibly do. But he had done it. From the lounge, I heard the housemother say, "Call your parents. School has been called off."

"One good thing. No Nat Sci exam tomorrow."

"Anyone driving to Chicago tomorrow?"

I had to get away. Upstairs in my dorm room, I grabbed my coat and was about to run for the door when my roommate came in the room.

"Did you hear what happened?" she asked.

"Yes. Yes, I heard," I said, moving past her.

"Where are you going?"

"I don't know," I said. "I don't know."

Once outside, I was sorry I had not taken time to put on my boots. Walking through snow in nylon stockings and black dress flats was cold, but I welcomed the stars and a world where people did not know about Herb, where there were people who had never met and would never know him.

I walked, trying not to think about Herb, but I kept seeing him sitting at his desk, putting the gun to his head. What did he think about during those last moments as he pointed the gun and then shot himself, while we were laughing and talking and eating our chocolate mousse?

Down the streets of Mount Carroll, Illinois, I walked. Through the lightly falling snow, I walked. The thin soles of my flat slippers covered only the bottoms of my feet, which had become frozen in the damn nylon stockings. Other students were walking in the opposite direction. First, I met Mike, who nodded; then walking up a steep hill, I saw Jenny, also walking alone, and, a block later, another friend, Steve. Four blocks later, I met a couple holding hands. Each time we nodded to each other, or said a muffled "Hi" but did not speak. We had come to be alone.

I set a goal—to realize what had happened, to face the reality of what Herb had done, because it seemed so impossible.

Down the streets, I walked—over the hills of the storybook little town that looked like an Illinois-modern Bethlehem, a college town where students did not use sidewalks, much to the dismay of its residents. Christmas lights, wreaths, and bright lawn decorations mocked the deep sorrow of the night.

I had no destination in mind, but I found myself near the Keohanes' gracious home. By now my feet were like blocks of ice. For a moment, I stood before the double door of the brick Victorian home of the sociology professor and then rang the bell. I expected friendly Mrs. Keohane, a high school teacher, a wise and sweet woman, to answer the door.

But instead, it was the blustery sociology professor, bald Mr. Keohane, who came to the door. I had no idea what I was going to say to him.

"My wife isn't here," he said gently, and then to my surprise, "Come on in." He held the double doors wide, or I probably would have turned away.

I stomped the snow from my shoes and took them off, then holding them, followed him to the kitchen. We both looked at my cold red feet. "You can warm your shoes over there," he said, pointing to a radiator. I placed my flats near the hissing radiator, sat in a kitchen chair, and kneaded my toes, bringing them back to some degree of warmth. Mr. Keohane filled the teakettle and began preparing tea. My toes assumed a brilliant, painful red by the time the teakettle whistled. He looked at me with sad, puzzled eyes as he brewed the tea. "It's too bad," he said. "It's too bad."

"Yes," I said.

The feeling in my toes had returned, and they hurt like hell. I found this man, whom I had always thought of as distant and gruff, strangely comforting.

"I'll be in the living room if you need anything," he said, and left me alone to sit undisturbed and drink the tea.

I sat there in the Keohanes' kitchen and thought about Herb; I tried to remember the sound, the melody of Herb's mopping-the-floor whistle. I thought of him sitting in our Irrational Man class, how he would stretch out and rock back on his straight back chair when an idea disturbed him and while he crafted a response. Had they already removed his body? He had always seemed so strong, but now he was weaker than weak—dead—like an immature baby bird that had emerged too soon from its broken shell. Was it the same with a soul as with a body? Could a soul, prematurely and violently hatched, survive?

Mr. Keohane came in and wordlessly poured more tea into my cup. I stirred some sugar into it. My feet were becoming warm, and my shoes seemed reasonably dry.

Without saying anything, Mr. Keohane left me alone again, giving me the time I needed to be able, once again, to deal with the world.

We all failed Herb, I thought, *desperately failed him,* and now we could never get him back. Once he had asked me for a date, and I had said no. I sensed he thought I didn't want to go out with him because he was black. I wanted him to understand that was not the reason; now it was too late.

I found Mr. Keohane reading in the parlor. I looked into his face, which bore the same puzzled, sad look as when I had come. "I think I'll go back now. Thanks for the tea," I said.

He nodded.

The door of the old Victorian house closed behind me as tightly as a cover on a box of Christmas chocolates. I was outside again, alone, breathing pure Mount Carroll winter oxygen.

"Where have you been?" my worried roommate asked as soon as I got back in our dorm room.

"Walking," I said.

"The dean has been calling for you," she said. "He's called twice. I didn't know where you were. I didn't know what to tell him."

"The dean's been calling me?"

She nodded.

"What does he want?"

"I don't know. He's in his office. Here's the telephone number. You're supposed to call him right away."

I went down the hall to use the dormitory telephone. "Hello," I said when he answered.

"How are you doing?" he asked.

"I'm okay. I'm fine."

"We have a problem," he said, which seemed a huge understatement. "All of us are worried about how Herb Taylor's death will affect the other students. We're dismissing school. We don't want any more...tragedies." I heard him take a breath. He continued, "Herb had a girlfriend, Rosie. I understand you are a friend of hers."

Rosie. Yes, Rosie. I had forgotten about Rosie. I hadn't seen her since dinner.

"She and Herb were very close friends," I said.

"Apparently they were more than friends."

"Oh?"

"We don't want her to be alone. There is some reason to believe that Herb's death may have been related to...well, anyway she's quite distraught. She's outside my office now. She's asking for you, or rather she's agreed to stay with someone, and she says she will stay with you. Are you willing to do that? Are you willing to stay with her? We have a room for the two of you in the dormitory. We'll see she gets home safely tomorrow."

"Okay. Sure." What Rosie had been going through these past few hours, I could not imagine. She wrote beautiful poetry, was uncompromising and fragile, estranged from her wealthy father who disliked Shimer and was threatening to stop paying her tuition. How could she go home to her family? I was surprised she had chosen me to be with her this dreadful night. In the fall, she had made fun of me when I wouldn't go hitchhiking to Chicago with her and Herb.

"Of course I'll stay with her."

Time slowed way down; it was only ten o' clock when Rosie and I climbed into the bunks of the stark dormitory room reserved for us. I felt I had been up for days. Unfortunately, the room was next to the pay phone, the only phone in the dorm capable of long-distance calls.

Almost the entire night, someone was on that phone calling home. "Mom? They're dismissing school. I'm coming home. Can you pick me up?"

"Herb Taylor killed himself, that's why. He was our star basketball player." Again, and again, they kept describing Herb as "our star basketball player." Basketball player. So what? It wasn't as if we had a good team. Shimer's claim to basketball fame was having the league's longest run of losses.

"I'll tell them to be quiet," I said.

"No, don't. I don't want them to know we're here. Anyway, they have to call home," Rosie reasoned.

I stayed on the top bunk and listened to Rosie cry into her pillow. Sometimes she would stop crying and we would talk, then we would lie there quietly, remembering Herb, then more talking, and again I would hear her sobbing.

Would the telephone conversations never stop?

"Can you come and get me? Please. Otherwise, I can't get a train until five o'clock tomorrow afternoon. This place is getting really spooky…Oh, thank God!"

"Yes. Yes. Herb Taylor. No, you never met him. Anyway, he shot himself in the head. Blew his brains out. Yeah, I don't know why. They said his family had some kind of mysterious disease."

"Is that true?" I asked Rosie.

"Yes, his family had a genetic illness. Men in the family became helpless invalids and died in their fifties. He thought the same thing would happen to him. The whole family was being studied by NIH."

"I didn't know." How little I really knew Herb.

"We were going to be married," Rosie said quietly, almost whispering.

Again, someone at the phone: "I don't know where he got the gun. I guess he must have had it in his room. They say he played Russian roulette."

Rosie responded without my asking. "Herb believed in fate. I can just see him point the gun to his head, asking…saying…if he and I were meant to be happy, he would live. If not—" She made what

114

sounded like a low sound, or perhaps it was a sob. "If it had been different, he would have been telling me about it tomorrow morning, and I would be saying…Oh God, Herb."

But it didn't go differently.

It was irrational, I thought. *Herb, it was really irrational.*

Before merciful sleep finally came, in the distance, across the quadrangle, I thought I heard Herb whistling, but of course, that couldn't be.

I turned to the wall and prayed to Whomever-Whatever could help. I prayed for Herb. Herb's suicide had left a big, long ugly tear in the fabric of the universe. I prayed for Rosie and asked God to help all of us get through this terrible night.

Following that evening, I was called on sporadically to help with Rosie, who completed her year at Shimer by drowning her sorrows with alcohol. Unfortunately she slept in a top bunk in the dorm and sometimes needed help getting to bed.

Then, on the first really beautiful day of spring while walking to downtown Mount Carroll, I saw Rosie on the sidewalk across the street. She was very drunk, and for the first time, I was furious rather than sympathetic. How could anyone get drunk on the first real spring day? The sun was shining! It was time for Rosie to get a hold of herself. I ran across the street to confront her.

"Rosie. What's the matter with you?"

She looked up at me, her eyes foggy and glazed. "They...buried Herb," she said slowly, mechanically, as if Herb were a dog bone. "I just came back. I needed a drink."

"They just had his funeral now?" I asked.

"They had to bury him...outside the Catholic cemetery," she said slowly, slurring her speech. "He wasn't good enough... to be inside...because... because ...suicide." The look of despair she gave me shattered all feelings of judgment as anger drained out of me. How could the church be so cruel?

"I'm....I'm so sorry," I said. I put my arm around her, and we walked back to campus together.

* * * * *

Irrational Man—the course Herb had instigated—and the books I read by Kierkegaard had a major effect on me. I was hungry to study theology. However, the church I grew up in, founded on the Grundtvigian principles of "Human First, Christian comes next," was in the process of merging with other Lutheran churches, which seemed alien to me. (I have since made my peace.) I was churchless. Women were not being ordained. Spiritually I was hungry; religiously I was lost.

I applied to the divinity school of the University of Chicago and was awarded a full tuition scholarship. Following college graduation, I married John Mitchell Martin; it seemed my destiny. He had left school and was now divorced, had given up so much for me, and loved me so much. He was taller and smarter than I, as well as handsome, funny, and charming. We were both in the first Timber Lake Playhouse theatre company in Mount Carroll, Illinois, near Shimer College before I began my studies. Unfortunately, John was not accepted at the University of Chicago graduate school. He got a job as an editor of textbooks at American Schools and enrolled for classes at Roosevelt University. I began my studies at the University of Chicago Divinity School. I was without church support; my family was puzzled about my enrolling in divinity school; John was openly critical and opposed to my schooling. After a year in which I loved attending classes and enjoyed fellow students, I willingly gave up my education and took a job in order for him to pursue his degree. Looking back, I am kinder with myself for that decision. Like other people, I need support.

Herb was right. Man is irrational—John's drinking was a problem I attributed to a Dylan Thomas–type of talent and sensitivity. I was unfamiliar with its destructive power. Woman is also irrational; I was not worried. I believed somehow life would work out just fine.

The world was becoming increasingly unsafe in the sixties, and the part Herb's life and his life-ending played in my life was just beginning.

Herb, the rest of Shimer's basketball
team, and a cheerleader.

9

Jack

"Carry your case record book like this," Leneta said, showing me how to carry my caseworker's black book in front of my chest. "No one will bother you. It's a sign to the Blackstone Rangers to leave you alone. They don't want anyone hurting a caseworker. The Rangers want the money white folks bring into the ghetto."

A mere two weeks of training along with a college degree in any subject had provided the necessary certification for me to become a caseworker for the Cook County Department of Public Aid. My most valuable training came from Leneta, my new friend, coworker, and mentor whose desk was next to mine.

Leneta had grown up in Mississippi and had lived in Chicago for several years. Black, smart, and stylish, she knew the ropes, considerably more than I did when it came to Chicago's South Side. Coming from a small town, I had no concept of the extent of urban poverty. As Leneta said with a hint of teasing, I was one of the "white folks." We became close friends and worked well together in our five-member caseworker unit in the special office on Maryland Avenue, only a few blocks from the University of Chicago.

One of the largest research studies on public welfare policy was being conducted in that office. The question being studied: does high quality professional counseling and attention make a sufficiently positive difference in the lives of public aid clients to justify the cost? To answer the question, the Chicago University research team had divided caseworkers into two groups. One group of caseworkers had master's degrees in social work. My group had college degrees in any discipline, and after two weeks of orientation, we were thrown into the water to see if we could swim. Caseloads in our group were about four time larger than the master's degree group and spread over a wide geographic area (47th Street to 63rd Street, Cottage Grove to Lake Shore Drive) compared to their limited caseload of approximately fifty cases in a confined area, often living on only one square block. The more professionally trained group worked with one kind of clientele while my group handled all types of cases: BD (Blind/Disabled), ADC (Aid to Dependent Children); OAA (Old Age Assistance) and GA (General Assistance).

The years 1963–64 were tough times in Illinois for both public aid clients and caseworkers. In a budget dispute, the state legislature stopped all payments to public aid recipients. Weeks went by while no one on public aid received a check. Unable to distinguish between the caseworker and the Illinois legislature, a welfare recipient shot one of the caseworkers—killing him. Another caseworker went a little crazy; standing on his desk, he yelled obscenities, threw case records around the room, and walked out.

* * * * *

On a cold November day, instead of sitting in a cozy classroom at the divinity school of the University of Chicago, I was "in the field" (a strange agrarian analogy) only a few blocks away from the classrooms I loved, and I had a decision to make. Should I risk being stuck in an unsafe elevator or take the equally dangerous stairs up four flights of a dilapidated tenement? Leneta had warned, "Don't take the elevators in that building."

Heeding her advice, I started up the stairs, which most likely had not been cleaned for years, finding traction between the piles of old dirt, crumpled papers, and discarded cigarette butts that littered the staircase. Lath-exposed walls jumped out at me like the ribs of hungry children amid the sick, stifling stench of old urine. Thank God it was a cold day.

I arrived at the second floor stairwell. On to the third floor. A few blocks away, the gray stone towers of the University of Chicago would have protected me from this reality.

Coming around the second bend toward the third floor, I met two older boys racing each other down, three steps at a time. I hugged my back against the wall and remembered a saying from Shimer College: *All experiments are successful; you always learn something. There is no such thing as a failed experiment.*

Third floor. I stopped for a rest. A skinny unshaved man, one eye bulging, the other covered with a patch, asked me for a cigarette. I shook my head and hugged my casework book in front of me. Thankfully, he walked away.

When I finally reached the top floor, I knocked on the door of the Warren apartment; I knocked and knocked. No answer. I knocked again.

"Whosat?"

"It's Mrs. Martin," I said. "Your caseworker."

After a few minutes, Thelma Warren unbolted the door and released the chain catch. Peering out at me through the eye that was not swollen shut, a scowling Thelma was obviously unhappy to see me. "Aww…Awww…C'min," she said reluctantly, inviting a necessary problem into her apartment, one which was remarkably clean but contained few furnishings, including only one bed. The little girl, Eugenia, the youngest of Thelma's three children, was missing her underpants, and the little boy was wearing a dirty adult T-shirt.

Thelma sighed, took some soiled clothing off the only chair, and motioned for me to sit down. I sat down and opened my case record book. Thelma sat on the bed.

"How are you doing?" I asked.

She shrugged her shoulders and made no reply. Thelma had a heavy Caribbean accent coupled with a speech impediment, and she spoke with a cadence that made it even more difficult for me to understand her.

"How is it going with Julian?" Julian, the oldest, was her eight-year old.

I was thankful he was in school.

"Baad. He very baad," Thelma said, "I cantah beat im anymoah. He git big sores, I canna'ta beat im."

Ezra, her middle child, looked at me, his eyes opened wide. Eugenia was hiding behind the bed, occasionally poking her head out to look at me. "I do whadyousay. I not beat im. Do no good."

"What are you doing now?" I asked.

"I do whatyousay. I lockimin za closet."

"In the closet? I don't want you to lock him in the closet! I didn't say to do that. Why? What did he do?" I asked.

"He baad. I sent him to store for bread, he threw"—she demonstrated his rebellious act, holding up a pretend coin and pretended to let go—"mah last quarter in sewah. I wanna to beatim, but I do wah youa say. Notbeatim. So I lock im inda closet."

"Oh, Thelma. I didn't say that. Don't do that. Don't lock him in the closet!"

"Why not? He baad. You said I cannotah beat im anymoh."

"Thelma, don't lock *any* of the children in the closet. Please. It's very bad for them."

She shrugged. I looked at Ezra, who looked at me vacantly. "Okay?" I said.

"I only lock Ezra."

"No. Don't lock Ezra either. Have him…have him sit in the corner if he misbehaves."

She shrugged.

"I…we need to take the children for health examinations."

"They not sick. They baad. They not sick."

"But Eugenia…" The little girl poked her head up and dipped back down. She had what appeared to be cigarette burns on her arms; it was the burns that had made me realize I needed to get help for this family. Something had to be done, and it was more than I could handle. "She all right. Ezra try to hurt her. Ezra try flush her down the toy-i-let."

"Flush her down the toilet?"

Ezra laughed.

"Yeah. I pull her outah."

I nodded. I had met with my supervisor about the difficulties in the family. Public Aid did not have a child abuse unit, but there were procedures to follow. "First," my supervisor had said, "before you can make any referrals, you must see that all the children have health checkups. You'll have to take each of them to the doctor. Nothing can be done until that has been completed. Make the appointments. You will need to request vouchers for taxi rides."

Now I had to let Thelma know. "I'm coming back next Thursday to take you and the children to the doctor for checkups. We'll take a cab," I said.

"No. I donawanna go. Won-go. Doh na wanna go."

"We need to go. We have to go."

I felt something move near my right foot, and looked down just in time to see a rat scurry away. I jumped up. "That... was a...a... rat!"

"Yeah," Thelma said sleepily.

"Rat." Ezra repeated and laughed.

Little Eugenia came from behind the bed. "Where's the rat?"

My body was pumping with adrenaline. "I need to go now. I'll be back on Thursday. Nine o'clock in the morning. Be ready!"

Gathering my casebook and purse, I gave the message as plainly as I could. "Have the kids dressed. Julian too. He'll need to stay home from school." Was there any possibility they would be ready? "I'll see you then."

"Bye," Thelma said, as if dazed.

As quickly as I dared, I ran down the stairs ignoring the overpowering stink. A young man was coming up the steps just as I was rounding the third bend of the staircase. Thankfully, he stepped aside. Reaching the ground floor out of breath, I headed to the building manager's office.

I rapped at the barred window and kept rapping until a heavyset woman with dyed red hair, false purple painted fingernails, and deep jowls appeared. She wore a bright orange flowered dress and had a long scar on her upper right arm from what must have been a knife cut.

"I want to speak to the manager!"

"I am the manager. What's the big deal, honey?"

"You have rats in this building. A rat went right near my foot."

"We don't have no rats. Where you see this rat?"

"In my client's apartment. Mrs. Warren's. There are young children up there. It's dangerous!"

"*Miss* Warren," the manager corrected me. "You up seeing her? Well, honey, we can't help it if Miss Warren leaves garbage all over. That's how the rats come in."

"Her apartment is on the fourth floor! The fourth floor!"

"I can't help it."

"And…and…the elevator is dangerous!"

The manager looked at me and shrugged.

"I'm going to report this building."

She cocked her head and smiled.

"You're getting paid well for her rent," I said.

"Miss Warren," she said, "is lucky to have a place to live."

"I'm going to notify the Chicago Housing Authority," I said, turning away, hoping not to reveal my sense of impending defeat. The Housing Authority was inconsistent. Some building complaints were immediately responded to; other reports went continually unheeded. This likely was one of them.

As I turned and hurried out the door, I heard her laughing. She found me amusing. Perhaps I was.

In the distance over the city-black snow, I could see the towers of the University of Chicago. *Aquinas, Augustine, Kierkegaard, Hegel, Martin Luther, Tillich,*

Barth, I thought, *What do you have to say to this?* None of them answered me.

Slowly, I began walking to my next assignment, carrying my case record book in front of my chest. My feet were aching with cold. I was so absorbed in thinking about the Warrens, wondering what I could or should have done, that it was a while before I became aware that people around me were upset. I could hear snatches of conversation:

"They did it. They killed our boy."

"I knew it. I knew somebody'd do it. They couldn't have it! No way. He too good. They gotta kill him."

I passed an old woman wailing and headed for a telephone, one of the few in the neighborhood that worked. The phone booth was empty; obscenities scrawled the narrow chamber. I picked up the phone, deposited a quarter, dialed the office, and asked to speak to Leneta.

"Something has happened down here." I began. "I don't know what it is. Somebody's been killed or something. I—"

Leneta interrupted. "Joy. It's the president. President Kennedy has been shot. In Dallas. We don't know how bad it is, but he was shot in the head. It isn't good."

"*What?* I...I thought someone from here had been killed. People...people are crying..." My own emotions began to erupt. "Oh no!"

My supervisor came on the phone, bureaucratic and professional. "You have heard about the president?" she said. "We don't have much information. You better return to the office. Yes, come back here right away."

"I have just seen the Warrens," I said. "Things aren't any better. They might even be worse. I have a couple of more visits to make."

"No, you need to return to the office."

I hesitated. I wanted to go home. Jack Kennedy shot in the head, his brain splattered. What did that leave in Camelot? How could something like that happen?

Leneta came back on the telephone. "They are saying…now they are saying he is dead." Her voice shook. "President Kennedy is dead."

I still wasn't convinced. It could be a rumor. When things like this happen, there are always rumors. "Are you sure?" I asked.

"It's on the news," said my supervisor picking up the phone, the sound of tears in her voice. "If you want to go home, that's okay. It is all over the TV."

We didn't have a television, but I did not want to tell her that. My husband and I could barely pay graduate school and household expenses, even though our rent was half the cost of Thelma's, actually less than anyone on my caseload. Winter was coming, but I still had not been able to purchase a pair of good boots. One of my clients had some very nice boots I envied; most of them had television sets. It was bizarre. But my place in the economy was temporary; my clients' situations seemed hideously permanent.

At the bus stop, I waited for the "Stony Island and 55th Street" bus.

Behind me, I heard someone say, "Our boy. They got our boy."

With others gathered at the corner bus stop, I waited for the lumbering bus to take us somewhere, anywhere to escape the oppressive heaviness that had descended, the death of fledging newborn hope, perhaps unfounded hope, but any hope is better than none. I felt a part of the Blackstone ghetto community as never before. A fertile egg of glistening hope had cruelly been aborted. They got our boy. Who were the "they" who got "our boy"? Was this someone's evil plan? What was it about our world that fostered such evil deeds?

The bus came; I got on board with the others, walked down the narrow aisle, and took an empty seat. Inside the bus, some people were gloomy, others related a theory about what had happened. Occasionally, I would hear a giggle, then an expression of despondency or words of supposed wisdom. Out of the window again, I caught a view of the ivory towers of the University of Chicago, which I had left only a few months ago. How irrelevant knowledge seemed, how impotent!

My mind turned to envisioning Kennedy's brain, a clever tangle of gray mass that had studied, thought, calculated, deliberated, solved, understood, and intended. His brain had helped him make his way through vast thickets of political and social intrigues, formulate decisions, develop strategies, compose speeches, create humorous insights. Now it was splattered. Like a first young love that is not to be, Jack would not have the chance to prove himself. But what struck me most was how personal this tragedy was in the ghetto. Even though Kennedy, the country's president, was a wealthy and powerful politician, a Harvard graduate married to a socialite, Jack Kennedy wasn't "white folks" like I was. Jack was "our boy." He was one of them. That meant more than any other eulogy that could be given. Jack was loved and believed in by the people who lived in one of the most miserable urban ghettos in the United States. "Our boy." And although I didn't live in the ghetto, I felt exactly the same way. I even felt some powerful "white folks" must be responsible.

Jack Kennedy was more than his brain, his abilities, his money, his body; that which was "the more" would survive. Of that I was confident. *What happened to you, Jack?* I wondered. *Where did you go when you left that hospital emergency room where you died, when you left your bleeding body in Texas?*

I pulled the chord to get off at the next stop. Was it one person's deed, or was there a conspiracy? My instincts were telling me there had to be more to this. But then when it comes to life-endings, there is always more happening than we understand. Nothing will ever change the impact of John Kennedy's death on the entire country. A person is much more than what he or she does. What is eternal is not a person's accomplishments no matter how grand they are— or might have been. What is eternal is the core of the person's existence, their being, their spirit. And thankfully, that cannot be killed.

Because I was in the ghetto on the day Kennedy died, I have associated the two experiences together. The Warren family, with whom I was visiting that day, was my most troubling case. I woke up at night, seeing those children, worrying they might be hungry. The older boy was truant from school and was in trouble for damaging someone's car. I had seen Ezra acting inappropriately toward his sister. I feared the burn marks on the little girl's arms must be made by the mother. I was at a loss of how to give any of them real help.

After going through all the necessary obstacles to obtain assistance—months of doctors' appointments, assessments, verifications, telephone calls, and rescheduling, I was told there were no services, no agency available to help, no waiting lists, and no more waiting lists for the waiting lists. Why then had we gone through all this if there was no help available? Because it was the procedure, that was why.

Then one day in the spring, to my amazement, Thelma came to the office to see me. I couldn't believe she had come all the way from her apartment; Thelma rarely went anywhere. What possibly could be the reason?

"I wanna tell you somethun if you promis not to tell nobody," Thelma said.

I looked at her newly swollen eye and bruised lip, thinking someone had hurt her.

"I can't promise that, Thelma."

"Then I canna tell yah," she said slowly and turned to leave.

"Tell me, Thelma," I said, stopping her.

"Yah gotta promis."

At first, I hesitated, but I needed to know. "Okay," I said. "I promise."

Thelma started to weep. "I…I tried to hang Ezra," she said.

I was shocked. I had thought she was going to tell me someone had beaten her.

She went on. "I got him up on the door, his head in mah belt. I hung the belt ovah the door, and I hung him there and then…then I look at im, and I think no…no, not kill Ezra. He baaad but not kill im. I cut im down."

"Oh, Thelma!"

"Nex time, I fraid ah won' cut him down."

I looked at the poor woman, and in spite of her terrible deed, I felt sorrier for her than I had felt sorry for anyone in my entire life. She had low intelligence, no education, a speech impediment, drank too much, and was desperately poor.

"Thelma, you need help. You have to get help. Now go back home. I'll do what I can. Call me if you have trouble with any of the children. Will you do that? Call me before you do anything to them."

She nodded.

Because a child's life was in danger, I had to tell my supervisor. I felt guilty for breaking my agreement I should never have made, but I couldn't handle this alone. My supervisor directed me to take Thelma to the psychiatric unit at Cook County hospital. There were no other resources available for Thelma or the children. Because she had no extended family, I had to sign papers to commit her. At first, I refused to do so, but it seemed there was no other way. After finally arranging child care, I took Thelma to the hospital, not sure it would help but knowing that something had to be done. She didn't understand what was happening. I left her there screaming obscenities at me. The relationship we had developed over the months was now in total ruins. I turned to the woman who had admitted her and asked what was going to happen to Thelma.

"Oh, we'll keep her for a week to scare her and then send her home. It usually does the trick."

I couldn't believe what I was hearing. "What do you mean? Aren't you going to help her?" But the admitting clerk ignored me. I nearly staggered out of the hospital. What had I done? What *had* I done?

A week later, I resigned. I felt I was being paid to do harm to people.

A year or so later, Cook County Department of Public Aid ended as a separate unit and became part of the regular State of Illinois program. A few years after that, special child abuse units came into being.

Looking back on it now, I am more compassionate toward myself. I believe that Thelma was asking for help, that she cared more about Ezra than what might happen to her. I admire her for coming to see me. Perhaps the person who answered my question about Thelma's care was kidding me, or didn't know better, but I doubt it.

The university's study? Several years later, a child welfare administrator familiar with the project told me the research had proved that people's lives definitely improved when more professional attention was given to the clients, but the cost-effectiveness was not definitive. An interesting finding was that both sets of caseworkers were equally stressed and discontented. The stress of human pain, whether fifty cases or two hundred, is equally difficult to handle.

Leneta moved to California, and we lost contact. I recall one of Leneta's observations in regard to the difference in racism between the North and the South. "In the South," she said, "people hate your race, but they love you as an individual. In the North, people love you for your race, but they don't love you as individuals."

Thirty-five years later, I asked my son whose job in Chicago provided him with computer access to extensive data on prison populations to look up Ezra Warren (not his real name). The report came back that he was in the Joliet prison on a long sentence for armed robbery. I was so proud of Ezra! At least he was alive and not in prison for rape or murder. I'm glad that I may have saved the life of an armed robber, even though he probably has cost the State of Illinois a lot of money. Perhaps if the Warrens had been in the other study group, things could have been even better.

As for Jack Kennedy, his death was the result of the high price we pay for free will, which enables human beings to do terrible things to other human beings for nefarious reasons, often for more money. The scar tissue from the Kennedy assassination continues to cause pain, which is what happens when there is incomplete healing. In spite of all the theories and studies, mistrust remains.

They got more than our boy.

10

Nelly

Before leaving my job as a Cook County case-worker, I made several required annual visits to several seniors—OAA (Old Age Assistance) clients. I recall several of the clients I visited, especially an old woman whom I will call Mrs. Easton. After knocking at her apartment door in a dilapidated high-rise and showing her my credentials, she began unfastening the several chains that secured her door. Mrs. Easton was missing a few teeth but in spite of this, was handsome and seemed quite able.

I couldn't help noticing a strong smell of perfume, which seemed strange. Nelly Easton didn't know me and obviously was distrustful, so once inside her apartment, I tried to make her as comfortable as possible so she would talk to me.

"You have some nice furniture," I said, looking around the apartment, which seemed considerably more cozy and pleasant than any other client's.

"These are gifts from my son," Nelly said, pointing to the couch and matching chair. "They were approved."

"It's very nice," I said. "May I sit down?"

Nelly nodded, looking carefully at me to see if I were going to cause a problem for her. "Two case-workers ago, they said it was legal. If I keep my son buying me things on credit, he stays out of trouble," she added.

I smiled at her. Nelly was purposeful and strong. In the corner of the room, I noticed an altar with candles burning.

"You have an altar," I said, looking at the five or six candles in glass jars; a strong odor of incense was coming from the curious display, an array of feathers and other odd items. Above the candles, there was a photograph of the Virgin Mary and several pictures of saints.

"Oh yes." She smiled. "I say a lot of prayers." Then she added quietly, "I know things." After studying me a moment, she added, "You are going to receive a great gift…a great gift."

"Oh, what might that be?" I asked, not believing it for a moment but wanting to engage her.

"I don't know, but it is a very great gift."

"Well, it's my birthday next week," I said, humoring her. "I'll probably get something for my birthday."

"No, it isn't that," she said. "It is much more."

"Well, that will be nice," I said. After asking her the usual questions, checking her rent receipts and assuring her that she could keep her furniture, I wished her well and stood up, preparing to leave.

"It will be a *great* gift," Nelly said emphatically as I said goodbye to her and she closed the door, chaining all the locks.

* * * * *

It was a year later while about to celebrate my daughter's first birthday that I realized that however strange Nelly Easton seemed that day, a very special gift had arrived about the time I had called on her. A week before my birthday, Rosie, Herb's girlfriend at Shimer, had given birth to a baby girl.

In early August that year, Rosie and another friend from Shimer College came to visit John and me in our Hyde Park apartment. Before Rosie left, she said she wanted to talk with us about something and would be calling me. They left, and we went to bed. In the middle of the night, I sat up and woke my husband. "I know what Rosie wants," I said. "She wants us to adopt her baby."

During the previous night visit, we had not talked about the birth of Rosie's child. I had thought it better not to bring it up unless she did. After Herb ended his life, Rosie suffered from deep depression and eventually quit college. From what we were told, for a while she had lived in a garage and burned black candles. Then she had met a Puerto Rican man whom she loved and had given birth to their child. That was all we knew.

A week later, Rosie called and came to see us again. She asked us to adopt her child who was in a Catholic orphanage. Rosie was still alienated from her parents and without work. Rosie had not yet signed away all her rights to her child, but would need to do so in a few weeks when the baby reached six months old. "Since I cannot raise her, I want you to," she said.

The orphanage was not optimistic about the baby being adopted. Illinois adoption laws in 1964 required that adoptive parents and the child share the same ethnicity, which in this case (Irish and Puerto Rican) would be difficult if not impossible. However, a private adoption could be arranged through the courts while Rosie still had rights. But there wasn't much time. If we were to adopt the baby, it was necessary to arrange the adoption before Rosie's rights were completely severed in a few weeks.

John had taught in a school for foster children and felt strongly that we should adopt the baby—we would be better parents than none, he reasoned. I was impressed that Rosie was taking responsibility for seeing that the child would have parents. I had quit my job as a caseworker. Also, I did not think I would ever give birth to a daughter, which for generations had rarely occurred in John's family. (As it turned out, I also was to give birth to two sons.)

During the next few weeks, I met with Rosie several times. I wanted to make sure she would not change her mind or regret her decision. My husband and I had not considered ourselves ready to have children, but we did plan to have a family. Was this a good idea? We conferred with a lawyer, family members, and a clergyman. My mother only asked that before we make a final decision, I visit the baby at St. Vincent's Orphanage in Chicago. I rode city buses to see her.

"I'll go and get her," said the nun in a business-like tone. The nun obviously did not consider my husband and I (non-Catholics) to be suitable prospective parents, but perhaps she too thought we would be better than no parents for the baby.

Sister returned in a few minutes holding an armful of an energetic baby girl. My heart leapt with excitement when I saw our daughter for the first time, a beautiful, sparkling, nearly six-month-old baby girl dressed in a red flowered dress with matching bloomers. A red ribbon fastened with Scotch tape was attached to her nearly bald head. Her eyes were brown and huge, her skin a beautiful olive color, her features delicate. But what was most amazing was *herself*, which was not at all like I had expected, having been told that very young institutionalized babies are passive. This baby was very much in present tense! If she could have spoken, she would have asked, "What took you so long? I've been waiting."

I took the baby in my arms. Would she be my first child? As I did so, the nun realized the baby's wristband had not been removed and quickly reached over to remove it. I protested, "Don't worry. We know the mother. She is a friend of ours." But

Sister was already removing the wristband. Just as she cut it, I looked and with shock, read the name on the band: *Baby Girl Taylor*. Rosie had given the child Herb's last name.

Baby Girl Taylor? This couldn't possibly be Herb's child. Nearly three years had passed since Herb died. While Rosie had gone through a terrible grief, she hadn't lost her mind. Surely Rosie knew who the father was, the man who helped her through her depression and grief.

"This is the baby's first time outside of the nursery," the nun said. "We named her Mary Jo. She's a fine baby—never gives us any trouble."

I nodded, knowing there were more than two hundred babies in Cook County Hospital's nursery still waiting for placement.

"She's beautiful," I said, not wanting to give her back to the nun, but Sister was in a hurry.

"I'll take her back to the nursery now," Sister said impatiently. As she whisked the baby away from me, Sister turned to me, "Well, at least she's been baptized!" she said.

I nodded. "I'll be back on Thursday afternoon, right after court."

"Bring some clothes with you. She leaves here with a diaper. That's all."

When I walked out of the orphanage into the broad daylight that September morning, my mind was filled with a list of preparations for a baby's sudden arrival. I was so excited that I nearly danced down the steps. But at the foot of the stairs, I stopped, remembering the arm band on the baby's wrist. Baby Girl Taylor? Herb Taylor. Did Herb have something to do with this? Did he know about it? Was he somehow involved? How could he be?

All I know is that out of Herb's suicide, with all its sadness and pain, something beautiful came into the world, and I am very grateful. John and I named our baby girl Thea Marie. The name *Thea* (pronounced Tay-ah) came from the musical "Fiorello," which we had seen a few weeks earlier at Timber Lake Playhouse, where we had been members of the first company. We checked the program we had saved, enabling us to spell our daughter's name correctly. *Marie* is the traditional name for girls in my family.

Obviously, the adoption laws in Illinois changed a few years later, and it is likely that Thea eventually would have been adopted. But I believe Thea Marie was meant to come to us. The universe has ways of allowing for things meant to happen—to happen. Granted, it is often a mind-boggling, heck of a complex route, but a simple event.

How would Mrs. Easton know what was happening? Just like any of us know—we become aware of the extraordinary, a blink of the eternal. She sensed it.

11

Martin

On April 4, 1968, James Earl Ray aimed a rifle at Dr. Martin Luther King Jr., who was standing on a balcony outside his motel room in Memphis, Tennessee, and killed him with a single shot, changing everything. Racism could no longer be ignored. The need to renounce our country's racism could no longer be left to one man and his followers. Racism would now be forever on our collective conscience, a responsibility of all to eradicate.

I can't say I was surprised, but I was shocked and worried. "Oh no! Now all hell will break loose." I felt sick to my stomach and disconnected as I stared at the black-and-white TV news.

My husband and I had left Chicago the fall of 1966 and moved to Davenport, Iowa, where John chaired the Humanities department in a private Episcopal prep school, St. Katherine's/St. Mark's. I taught part time—Theater as Literature, Basic English—and also directed a play. I was pregnant when we arrived in Iowa, and in the spring, our son Lee Mitchell was born.

Thea entered the campus preschool at age 2 ½, where the early education program included music and French lessons. We lived in a pleasant brick house on campus midway up a steep hill overlooking the Mississippi River, with a pathway to the top of the hill where the main Victorian campus was located. Isolated in the city of Davenport with a new baby, I finally learned to drive.

Life was not idyllic. I did not yet admit that John was an alcoholic, but occasionally he would disappear in the middle of the night, and when he returned in the morning, he obviously had been drinking heavily. Nevertheless, our lives went on as if nothing was wrong. It helped that he would also go for weeks or even months without such an episode. His students loved him, and we enjoyed teaching.

Martin Luther King once said:

> All life is interrelated…somehow we're caught in an inescapable network of mutuality tied in a single garment of destiny. Whatever affects one directly affects all indirectly. For some strange reason, I can never be what I ought to be until you are what you ought to be. You can never be what you ought to be until I am what I ought to be. This is the interrelated structure of reality.[1]

The murder of Martin Luther King affected all of us. I wanted to *do* something about racism and poverty—not *be* "just" a wife, mother and teacher. In the days that followed, I attended the Dr Martin Luther King Jr. community memorial service and for the first time in my life, went on a peace march in Davenport. I brought a stroller for Thea, and off we went while my husband stayed home with our baby son, Lee Mitchell, named for the confederate general. (Lee's paternal great-grandparents were of southern persuasion; their three sons were named Robert, Edward, and Lee.)

The day after the march we returned to our daily lives—John to his classroom, me to caring for Baby Mitch and teaching in the afternoons, Thea to her preschool class.

* * * * *

"It's time for show-and-tell," Miss Tyler announced to her class. "Who has what to tell us this morning?"

Thea sat very still; she didn't like speaking up in class. Next to her, Sara waved her arm frantically, but Miss Tyler ignored her. "Thea, do you have something for show-and-tell?"

Thea shook her head.

"You think about it," Miss Tyler said. "I'll come back to you. Sara?"

"We have a new puppy!" Sara said proudly.

"A new puppy! What's the puppy's name?"

"Charlie."

"Charlie, that's nice. And what kind of dog is he?"

"He's... a...a mutt!"

"Well, we're going to have a Pet Open House in the Spring. Maybe you can bring Charlie?"

Sara nodded and sat back in her chair, satisfied.

"Now, Thea," the teacher said, "is there something you can share with us?"

Thea stood up. "The king died," she said softly. "We walked all over."

"What king? Oh, you mean, Martin Luther King? You went on the peace march?"

She nodded.

"That was a very long walk, wasn't it? Do you children know who Martin Luther King was?"

"He got shot dead!" Bobby answered.

"Yes that's true. But who was he? Do you know, Thea?"

"He was the king," Thea said, thinking of the cartoon kings she watched on Saturday mornings.

"Why did someone shoot him?" Laura Jean asked.

"Some people do bad things," Miss Tyler explained. "Martin Luther King believed we should treat everyone alike, that it doesn't matter if someone has a different skin color from your own. He taught us to accept people who look differently."

"So he got shot!" Bobby said, pointing his finger like a gun.

"Bobby, that's enough!" Miss Tyler said.

* * * * *

"I don't want to go to bed. I don't!" Thea frequently didn't want to go to bed, but the last few days, her behavior had become different, downright difficult.

"Sorry, it is already way past bedtime," I said. I took her hand, and when that didn't work, picked her up and carried her up the stairs. Thea was crying; she kicked me in the stomach.

"Hey. That hurt! Don't wake your brother," I said, but it was to no avail. She let out a howl. I kept walking up the stairs, carrying her in my arms. In her bedroom, she refused to cooperate in putting on her favorite pajamas. Her small body jerked so much it was difficult to get the pajamas on her. I was getting tired of all this.

"Okay. Let's have a story," I said.

"I don't want a story."

"You sure you don't want a story?" Thea shook her head, tears streaming down her face.

"All right. Why don't you tell me a story?"

She looked at me, puzzled. The tears stopped, then after a moment of hesitation, she started crying again.

"Thea, stop it. What's wrong?" When we had adopted her at six months, she didn't cry at all, even when soap got in her eyes. Crying had been a breakthrough to be celebrated, but now she was becoming almost hysterical. I sat down, picked her up, and put her in my lap. "What's the matter? What *is* the matter?"

She continued to sob, but stopped thrashing. I finished buttoning her pajamas. Sitting in the big wicker rocker holding Thea on my lap, I began rocking. "It's okay. Whatever it is, it is going to be all right."

Thea's swollen eyes closed for a moment. She spoke so softly I could hardly hear her. "Bobby says…Bobby says I'm going to get darker and darker. That I'm black and that Nicky won't be my friend anymore." There, it was out. She sobbed, turning her face away.

"He said WHAT?" I stopped rocking her and looked at her in disbelief. "What else did Bobby say?"

She struggled, almost choking. "Bobby said that when you find out…you'll give me back." Having now told all, she muffled her cries against my chest, catching her breath again and again.

I didn't say anything for a few moments. I was too angry—at Bobby and even more at his parents for perpetrating this hatred. After someone had the gall to shoot Dr. Martin Luther King, instead of coming to their senses, adults were visiting their bigotry on their young children! Hatred and racism had invaded my home and hurt my child.

I understood Thea needed to cry it out, so we simply rocked. I doubted she really believed we would give her back. She was too smart for that. But that little stinker Bobby had created a doubt in her heart and soul about her place in the world.

Finally I said, "Bobby is wrong. To be exact, you are half Puerto Rican, which is made up of all kinds of colors—black, white, brown—and you are also half Irish. Anyway, what color you are doesn't make any difference. You like Josie. She's your friend, isn't she?"

Thea nodded.

"Josie is black. We don't care what color you are. Not one bit. You are our daughter."

She huddled closer. "You belong to us—black, white, brown or purple. What matters is being a good person. We love you just the way you are."

I had a different Danish lullaby for each of my children, with special words for each of them. Hers was "Nightingales of the summer night are singing for little Thea." That night, we rocked a while longer. But before she fell asleep, she raised her head to ask, "Could you…Could you…make your hair brown?"

"I'll see," I said, admiring her spunk. Thea wanted me to change.

Back downstairs, I expressed my anger, telling John what had happened. Bobby's father owned the largest real estate company in town. What kind of person was he? I could only guess. "I want to pull her out of that preschool. I don't want my daughter exposed to children like that!"

"Cool it," John said and reminded me that Thea was attending an excellent preschool with free tuition because we were on the school's faculty.

"I don't care. I don't like it. What does Bobby say to Josie? How is it affecting the kids? I'm going to talk to the teacher tomorrow."

"Things are going to change now. The death of Martin Luther King will make a difference," my husband said. "You'll see."

* * * * *

King's last words on the balcony prior to his assassination were a request for a musician/friend scheduled that night to sing "Take My Hand Precious Lord." He seemed to have a premonition that his death was imminent. Whenever I hear that song, I think of Dr. Martin Luther King. *"Through the storm, through the night, lead me on to the light, Take my hand, precious Lord, lead me home."*[2]

The end of Martin Luther King's life affected our lives. It didn't stop racism, but it did change things. Toxic racism divides us as a people of the earth, and it must be overcome in order to advance us as a civilization; it is a necessary hurdle in evolution.

King always knew his life and death would be a catalyst for change. The violence that erupted over the murder of this nonviolent man became a catalyst for the Great Society program, an effort to wipe out poverty in the United States.

* * * * *

Two years later, we left St. Katherine's/St. Mark's School; John obtained a job as a newspaper reporter for the *Rock Island Argus*. Doubts about our future had begun to trouble me. His alcoholism had advanced, and I knew I needed to be economically independent and able to support the family. But I was again pregnant. In September 1970, after a record seventeen-day rain, our son Noah was born. (The name had been chosen months prior to his birth, but he made the front page of two newspapers as the possible cause of the endless rain.) After Noah was born, I was determined to have a "real" job.

In the city of Rock Island, Illinois, across the Mississippi River from Davenport, community leaders from the academic, local government, and business communities came together to "do something" about racism and poverty. With help from the federal government, a "bad" neighborhood on the west side of Rock Island was declared a Model City and awarded a five-million-dollar grant over five years (real money in 1970). The area would be a model for alleviating poverty and racism by developing and providing comprehensive services in the neighborhood.

John did not want me to work. At first, he said I couldn't get a job because I had no qualifications, and if I did get one, the cost of child care would exceed what I could make. There was a bigger problem. If I worked, John said our family's survival would no longer depend on him; my getting a job would encourage his alcoholism. I still believed our marriage would somehow work out, but also realized I had to get a job, even if he greatly opposed it.

I obtained a job at Model Cities and went to work when Noah was six weeks old. "I know a lot of people who went to Shimer. I never met anyone who graduated," Phil Auffrey, my new boss said, who was impressed by my education. He hired me with the

consent of the city of Rock Island's city manager, cit-
ing my combined experience both as a caseworker and
a teacher. I was a "social planner" and in a year, when
Auffrey left, became chief planner of the Rock Island
Model Cities program. I involved myself deeply in
my work, working with the community to establish
and fund a legal aid center (the first in Rock Island),
a new child development center for low-income children, a mental health center, and a new health center
which, for the first time, included family planning,
and many other ventures. Today, the neighborhood is
still poor, but "The Martin Luther King Community
Center" and several community services that began
with the Model Cities program continue.

Then, in 1972, Richard Nixon became president, and the dismantling of Model Cities began.
The Great Society, soldiers in Vietnam, my marriage,
and my father were all dying.

When I received the phone call at work notifying me of my father's death, my work at Model Cities, which had seemed so important, seemed far less significant. My father's life-ending came with a new look at life and a direct encounter with life after death.

PART III

New Perceptions and Other Dimensions

12

Harald

Moving from room to room throughout the downstairs of the colonial-brick parsonage, Asta hurriedly closed windows. In the kitchen, she looked out, eyeing the root cellar a few feet away from the house. Surely the coming storm would not warrant a trip down there! Still it was comforting to know it was available if necessary. From a living room window, Asta could see the steepled white country church standing its holy ground in front of a dangerous amber-and-eggplant-colored sky, foreshadowing a major Nebraska storm. After a hot, fry-an-egg-on-the-sidewalk July afternoon, the air had turned alarmingly chilly. Tree leaves shook nervously in expectation.

Asta knew well that every ten years or so, a tornado would make an unwelcome visit, ripping through the prairie. Like a nasty giant-child, it would whimsically toss cattle and farm machinery into the air, dismantling houses and barns as if they were temporary sand castles. It was only a question of how fearsome this tantrum would be, how great its destruction.

No lightning. No thunder. A foreboding darkness settled over house and churchyard, as if to separate them from the rest of the world. Now small branches were moving back and forth like delicate fans mounting in intensity. Asta knew it would not be long before whole trees would sway back and forth, wavering, dancing feverishly, as if they might pick up their roots and completely run away.

Harald, pastor and husband, had gone outside to put their car into the garage, check garden equipment to see it was all safely stored, and move lawn chairs and the Weber grill inside the garage, to prevent them from being scattered into the next county.

Although Harald was ten years older than Asta, he was still strong and athletic. He had been a gymnast as a young man and a sportsman all his life. Asta was proud of how he continued to excel in sports and enjoy physical labor.

The summer of 1962 had been uncomfortably hot, but also a very special time for them. The couple had married off one daughter, sent the other to Europe, and enjoyed the heady experience of holding their first grandchild, Laura, the daughter of their son and his wife. Now Asta and Harald were planning retirement, a special time to enjoy life—just the two of them.

*****

The storm hit with a body slam. Wind churned, swirling dust through the air. The eggplant sky lost its amber color, becoming a muddy river-bottom brown. Asta looked out of the window as an aluminum side table, belonging to their set of lawn furniture, flew by. Ping-pong-ball-sized hail beat down on the sidewalks. and Asta could hear the sound of them hitting metal.

Where was Harald? She watched the hail bounce off the pump near the driveway. *Oh, the tomatoes*, she thought. *I hope it doesn't ruin the tomatoes. And what about the corn?*

Farmers could not stand one more summer of failed crops. It would only be a short while until harvest. Why now? Could the corn survive this latest onslaught of nature? They needed rain but this was coming down too hard. If only this hail did not last long. And where was Harald? He must have taken shelter in the garage. Surely he would not have headed into the root cellar without her.

Pools of rain gathered in the driveway. Asta watched the water rush down the gravel driveway between the house and the church—small rapids forming instant canyons ended in fairy-size lakes in the middle of the road. Now the rain was coming down with such force that she could see neither the garage nor the church.

The garage! Harald must have found refuge there, rather than try to make it to the house. If he tried to come now, he would be soaked to the skin!

Through the translucent wall of rain, Asta tried to make out a large form slightly moving on the other side of the lawn, a ghostly shape she could barely see, like some kind of animal. No, it was Harald! He was on the ground in the rain; hail was pounding his body. What…what had happened to him?

No one was around to help. She hesitated only long enough to grab a summer jacket. Shaking all over, Asta pried open the door against the wind and burrowed her way through surges of rain water and hail. She had to reach him. He must have fallen, hurt his leg or something.

Through pools of standing water up to her ankles, rain slashing her face, Asta made her way calling his name, "Harald! Harald!" until she reached his side.

Harald lay there in the soaking grass, his body slightly turned in order to avoid a direct current of water in his eyes. He looked at her and made strange guttural sounds, unable to speak. Asta huddled near him, trying to protect him with her body from the worst of the downpour. The rain was soaking them both; hail bounced off their bodies. Harald's gray-blue eyes looked startled to see her. Threads of dark corn-silk hair crisscrossed his nearly bald head. His face was strangely twisted, half smile, half scowl; his neck was large and swollen.

"I …fell…the…graaage…" was what she thought he said.

She knelt down and managed to put one of his arms over her shoulder. "We've got to get you up," she said. But she could not lift him. "C'mon," she cried in desperation.

"Mah… left… leg," he struggled to say. And then Asta understood; he had no strength on his left side. A stroke. Harald must have had a stroke. He was too heavy for her to lift. She must become his left side. If he could use the strength he had on his right side, she could get him inside the house. The hail slowed.

Like strange attached creatures, Asta and Harald began to move through grass dotted with balls of white ice freezing their hands and knees as they made their way. The hail stopped; the rain was heavy but no longer pounding, making it easier for Asta to see. With Harald's arm around her neck, she pulled him along with her, steadily moving slowly for thirty-odd feet toward the house—stopping, breathing, resting, moving again, silently crawling and crawling. Finally they arrived at the sidewalk, a highway to the house, but continued to make their way alongside it on the wet grass.

Reaching their cement back porch, Asta was relieved, but she could barely see because of the rain streaming from her hair down to her face. Her knees pained her, her shoulders ached, and her weak back could hardly bear the pain. She looked at Harald, who was white and strangely stiff. Half his face still smiled at her, striking a direct blow to her heart.

Not now, she thought, *don't get sick and die now. Don't you dare! Not just as the children are out of college and grown. Not now.*

She turned, and together they moved his torso until he sat draped on the bottom stair leaning on the iron porch railing. Asta managed to join him on the stair. She huddled with him, feeling the warmth of his body, both familiar and strange in its fragility. For several minutes, they sat together in the rain catching their breaths, then hearing a long crash, looked just in time to see their favorite oak come crashing down on the driveway.

He looked up at her and tried to speak, but faltered. She hugged his shoulders. "We have to get you inside!" Asta turned away and then stood up.. It was a miracle to stand upright. She was able to prop open the door against the complaint of the wind. Then she knelt beside him again, and together in a pull-push motion, first Asta and then Harald with her help, crawled inside the kitchen door.

It was wonderfully dry inside. She sat for a moment on the linoleum. Harald sat by the door, propped up in the corner, looking like a clothes-soaked drunk. Should he be lying down? She did not know. She wanted to sit and celebrate the accomplishment of shelter, but she knew she needed to get help as soon as possible. She reached for a dishtowel, began drying his face, moving cautiously, fearfully over his partial paralysis. She dried his hands. His limp left arm hung uselessly at his side, and she was too frightened to cry. Asta would have dried her own face, except the towel was now too wet.

Harald struggled and tried to get up.

"Stay there!" she said. "Don't move! I am going to call the doctor!"

"I wan… my… pipe."

"Your pipe???" she said. "No. No pipe! Now, don't move!"

"Pipe," he said.

She stood up and headed toward the telephone. In the hall mirror, her image—worried wet face and matted hair—was barely recognizable. How could she possibly meet the challenges confronting her? No time to think about it. She dialed 911.

"I need an ambulance. My husband has had a stroke."

"I'm very sorry. All our ambulances are out. There is a full-blown tornado between Grand Island and Aurora."

"We need help! My husband has had a stroke! He needs to be in a hospital."

"I can send a hearse if you like. That's all that's available."

"A hearse? Okay, send a hearse!" She gave directions.

"Harald had a stroke?" Someone asked over the party line. It was Herman, their neighbor.

"Yes," she said, feeling the sting of hot tears on her cold face.

"I'll be right over."

As she hung up the phone, she saw that somehow Harald had managed to stand and was staggering, wet and wobbly across the dining room. "My… pipe," he struggled to say as he came across the room and then fell on the dining room table, busting it in two. Harald and walnut table pieces came crashing down together.

"Oh no!" she cried, running to him. She knelt and bit her lip as she cradled his head. Harald was bleeding from his forehead, his brow scraped from the fall. She stood up again and went to find a quilt, covered him just as their party-line neighbor came up the lawn on his tractor.

"How is he?" Herman asked as he stepped inside the house.

"He's had a stroke. Can you help me move him?" At Herman's suggestion, Asta stuck an unlit pipe in Harald's mouth, and together the two assisted Harald to the living room sofa, where he lay down quietly. Only after he fell into a fitful sleep did Asta remove the pipe.

Asta knew it would take quite a while for the hearse to come. Two trees had blown down in their own driveway; the roads were not clear. Getting to a hospital right away would be impossible. For more than an hour, they waited, but at last the black hearse drove up the driveway as far as it could go. Herman ran out to meet it while Asta sat with Harald.

It is strange, Asta thought, a half hour later while sitting next to the driver in the front of the hearse on the way to the hospital, *very strange, to put your living husband in the back of a hearse.* Sometime in the future, she hoped they could pretend it was funny. As for now, Harald didn't seem to mind. This was Nebraska, and they needed help. One must make do.

*****

My father's incredible recuperative powers were amazing. In the remaining ten years of his life, Harald Ibsen managed to recover from two additional strokes, three heart attacks, three heart failures, a broken hip and a severe bout of infectious hepatitis, among other health issues. When he landed in the hospital with kidney failure, a doctor on call asked if he had been given the wrong medical chart—my father's medical history did not seem to match his condition.

At least three times, a doctor walked with me down the hall and told me quietly there was little hope that my father would recover. Each time Dad managed to come back.

*****

One night I came home after an especially traumatic time where my father had survived another round in intensive care. Thea, then seven years old, was still awake. I knew she was worried about her grandfather. I went into her bedroom and sat down beside her.

"Bedstefar [grandfather] is much better," I said. "He's going to be okay."

She looked up at me from beneath the covers. "I know," she said confidently. "I healed him."

Startled, I said, "That was good."

Two days later while visiting my recuperating father, I said, "Thea says she healed you."

"She probably did," he answered.

* * * * *

In January of 1972, Dad had yet another heart attack. This time, the doctor was emphatic. It was up to me to give my mother the news.

"The doctor wants me to talk to you about Dad," I said. Mother nodded and bit her lip, guessing what was coming. We sat together in the guest bedroom of their retirement home while the children played in the living room. Mother sat wearily on the bedspread, one that had been hand-knit by my grandmother. On the wall was a large portrait of herself as a bride in a long white satin wedding dress, carrying a dozen red roses—thirty-six years ago.

"The doctor says that if Dad does make it this time, he will be helpless. They say he is a 'Cardiac 5.'" Lifting his head off the pillow or putting on his socks could cause his heart to fail. He will need to have oxygen near him all the time. The doctor says six months at the very most."

Mother held my hand. Then she asked me to read Psalm 36.

* * * * *

But again, my father triumphed over most of the doc's predictions. He only used oxygen at home and seldom. By Easter, he was lifting up his two-year-old grandson, Noah, with whom he had a special bond. Together, the two of them reminded me of Mathias and my brother David a generation ago. That special bond between an old man and a young boy-child—I could only touch to its truth and simplicity—was the handing down of a spiritual torch.

In June, Asta and Harald went on vacation, returning to Nebraska. Back in Kronborg, Dad walked around the cemetery surrounding the country church across from the parsonage where he had his first stroke. He turned to his friend Hans, who had driven him out there.

"This would be a good place to rest," he said. "Can we go back to Central City over the old bridge?" he asked. Hans drove my father one last time over a rickety one-lane bridge straddling the Platte River, which is almost as wide as Nebraska skies. Wordlessly, one more time, they admired the corn-and-wheat-laden prairie glowing, growing in the bright summer sun. They passed old red barns, white farmhouses, singing windmills, and my father's favorite sight—a herd of white-faced cattle. Harald was saying good-bye to his world.

When I got the call in my office at Rock Island Model Cities, I put the phone down in disbelief.

What a way to go, I thought. I was so proud Dad had died on vacation, on the prairie, among people he loved.

* * * * *

This time, Dad's ride in the hearse was no joke. Around nine o'clock in the evening, most of the visitors had left the funeral home. Our exhausted family gathered in a little room next to the casket. It was a welcome respite. My husband sat next to me. Across from me, my pregnant sister Karma sat stiffly, stoic silent tears streaming down her face. My brother David seemed ill at ease. Mother was already trying to emotionally prepare for the funeral tomorrow. Her good friend, Hans's wife Sena, sat next to her, holding her hand. We were saying the usual things, how good it was to see everyone, exchanging and matching names with faces of visitors.

I sat quietly a few minutes. I was tired and did not want to talk to anyone. After only a few moments, I looked up, aware my father was in the room. His body was to my left in the casket; his spirit was to the right. We began a mental conversation.

Take care of Asta, he said.

In all those years of illnesses, we had never spoken about his dying or taking care of my mother.

Yes. Yes. Of course we will, I answered. How would my mother ever get along without him, I wondered. They seemed like one person. How alone she would be!

I have always loved all of you, he said.

It really is my father, I thought. His accent and pattern of speech were unmistakable.

I miss you, Dad, I said mentally. *I miss you so much!*

I have always loved all of you, he said again.

I know. How is it? How are you? I asked, glad he was alive—he was not imprisoned in that casket. He was without pain, without age.

I have seen so many of my friends today, he said.

It was as if he had gone to a wonderful reunion—like the old church conventions he liked to go to. I didn't think to ask him who he had seen. Instead I asked, *Did you know that you were going to die?*

Yes, I knew it that day, he answered.

His light-shaped disembodiment, which I could see so clearly, reminded me of a *Starship Enterprise* encounter. He moved over by my brother, as if concerned about him. But I was worried about my tearful sister, Karma. I wanted to ask about the baby she was expecting. Her first child had Down syndrome, and she was understandably anxious about her second pregnancy.

Will Karma's baby be all right? I asked mentally.

Yes, he assured me, *it will be all right.*

While his answer could mean many different things, I felt satisfied. *It will be all right* was said with my father's peculiar inflection of certainty. When he said something that way, it was always true.

Take care of Asta, he said again.

I will, I answered mentally. Again he had moved over by my brother, as if to give him a special blessing to help him.

I have always loved all of you, he said again.

John, my husband, was asking me a question, interrupting my concentration. I tried to stop his attempts to interrupt me. Finally, I mumbled, "Please be quiet. I'm talking to my dad."

He looked surprised for a moment, then nodded to where my father hovered behind my brother. "Is that him over there?"

"Yes. Please be quiet," I answered, grateful my husband, neither religious nor given to fantasy, could "see" him.

Can we talk again? I asked my father. I didn't want to let my father leave; he was fading from me.

Not very often, he said. *It wouldn't be a good thing.*

I didn't know whether what he said pertained to me, or whether it was a general admonition.

I miss you so much, I said in my thoughts. *I'm so glad you're all right.*

He seemed so young.

But I never "talked" to him again. However, I have felt his presence, and I never again doubted life in the hereafter. My dialogue with my father was more than a glimpse of eternity; it was at least a glance. Our energies are best centered on this life rather than the next, but what we believe about the "hereafter" or "thereafter" greatly affects how we live and what is important to us.

What about the "before-now"? I had always accepted some idea of life-after-life, I had never believed in life-before-birth. I was soon to see it as a possibility.

Harald Ibsen with blue jay friend

13

Ozzie

Excerpts from the local newspaper dated
September 1972:

Oswald (Ozzie) Bernhardt III, age
17, died yesterday from injuries
suffered after being run over by a
hit and run driver in the 1200 block
of Main Street at approximately 10
pm on Tuesday night. Bernhardt
was on his way home from a Central
High School basketball game and
apparently tried to cross the busy
street mid-block when he was run
over by a passing car. Witnesses
reported seeing a 1970 white sedan,
possibly a Buick or Oldsmobile, speed
away from the accident. Police are
asking the driver of the car to come
forward immediately. Ozzie was the

son of Dr. and Mrs. Peter Bernhardt
of Bettendorf. Dr. Bernhardt is
a well-known psychiatrist in the
community. A reward of $20,000 for
information leading to the arrest of
the driver is being offered by friends
of the family.

A teenage boy walking home from a basketball
game is run over by someone who didn't even stop?
How horrible! How tragic! I studied the photograph
of the young man in the paper—a sandy-haired boy
with freckles who seemed to peer back at me. He had
a slight, almost teasing smile and incredible light-col-
ored eyes—a beautiful young man! Now he would be
an eternally young memory. What a shock it must be
to his family. Lots of teenagers cross in the middle of
a street, but Main Street was a thoroughfare. Still, it
was ten o'clock at night; there should not have been
much traffic. How would his parents ever recover
from losing their son like that—no warning, no reason? How does a person survive losing a child?

My three children, ages 3 to 9, were outside
playing in the wet snow after a late springtime snow-
storm had unexpectedly descended the night before.
To their delight, their father was playing with them,
a rare treat. They were having a good time. It was an
opportunity for me to accomplish necessary household chores: laundry, vacuuming, and a long check-
list of other duties that needed tending before the
work and school week began again.

Looking out through the leaded living room windows, I saw the kids and John rolling a huge snowball. I made myself vacuum the living room and dining room carpets but couldn't shake the downhearted feeling I had since reading about Ozzie Bernhardt. It weighed on me even though I didn't know either him or his parents. Why was I taking this so personally? I wanted to weep.

I picked up the basket of whites waiting for me in the hallway and carried them down the basement steps. I made my way to the far corner of the damp, cold basement, turned the settings of the washing machine to "hot" and "super," and tossed in soiled underwear, socks, towels, and white shirts. As water filled the tub, I added a cup of bleach and the latest on-sale laundry soap. It didn't help. My mind went back to Ozzie. What was he like? Shy? Athletic? Quiet? An extrovert? I wished I knew something about him. Being the son of a psychiatrist probably wasn't easy. I shut the lid of the washing machine and went upstairs.

But by the time I reached the first floor, I felt very weak and cold. I decided to have a cup of tea, then changed my mind; I couldn't wait for the water to boil. I needed to lie down for a few minutes. It could be that I was coming down with the flu. John and the kids would be coming in soon. I would take advantage of the blissful quiet before they came back in the house. In the living room, I sank into our large overstuffed brown sofa and pulled up a soft green knitted afghan, almost covering my ears. Turning into the sofa's back, I tried to comfort myself. I was so very cold. I pulled the green afghan tighter around me, snuggled into a near fetal position, and drifted away. I either fell asleep or slipped into another space and time.

* * * * *

I saw a single chair in an otherwise empty room, then became aware of a woman gathering a shawl around her. "I am going out," she said.

"Please don't go. Please don't, Mama." There was someone else in the room, a little boy about four years old with deep brown eyes and his head covered with soft brown curls.

"I have to go," the woman said, "I'll be back." She spoke sternly to the child. "Don't cry. I will be coming back, but I must go. I need to get some food."

But the little boy cried out, "Please let me come with you. I don't want to stay here. It's cold. Please… Please, Mama." He pulled on her dress, desperate.

The woman pulled his arms away and turned from him. "Stop it! Stop your crying! I can't take you with me! I have to go. I will be back soon. I promise! I have to get us something to eat, and you have to stay here! Be brave, like a little soldier. I have to go!" She turned and left as he alternately wailed then tried to stifle his tears. Without glancing back, she quickly opened the door and shut it behind her. The little boy sat down on the floor and sobbed.

The woman walked and walked. In her thin wrap, she walked a long distance until she arrived

175

in another part of the city where there were tall gas street lights. She turned down a particular block; picking up the pace, she walked past large elegant homes. Finally, she stopped before a brownstone and resolutely climbed the stairs. The woman hesitated, uncertain or nervous, and then used the brass knocker on the door.

After a few moments, a man servant, almost as stout as he was tall, opened the door. He stared at her. "What are you doing here?" he asked haughtily. "You know you are not to come here."

"I need to talk to him," she said. "We are hungry."

Behind the servant, a female voice asked, "Who is it?"

"No one," the servant said, looking straight at her, an intruder. "No one."

"He promised me," the woman said urgently. "We have nothing to eat. Please."

"Wait here. Do *not* ring the bell again."

The heavy wooden door closed with the finality of a coffin lid. The woman stood outside the door, waiting. She waited and waited. She dared not move.

No one came. Still she waited. She waited so long that finally when there was a crack in the door she was startled to see his deep brown eyes looking down at her as if she were a miscreant.

"Go away," he said. "Don't come back again."

"I…I can't go away. We have nothing. We will starve. You said…"

"I said, if you come back, I would never help you again. And it appears you have come back."

"I had no choice. We're hungry. You promised...Your son...Think of your son."

"I have no son. You are never to come here again. Do you understand?"

"A loaf of bread. Just a loaf of bread. Please. I...I beg you."

But he had already shut the door.

For several moments, the woman continued standing there. Finally, hardly able to move, she stiffly turned and stumbled down the stairs to the gate, walking aimlessly. Her feet had become as numb as her heart. Tears froze unshed in her eyes. Where could she steal something to eat? She had never stolen anything in her life. What if she were caught?

At the street corner, the woman paused. A team of horses pulling a carriage with lanterns was coming down the street much too fast. She did not intend to do it, but a deeper part of her recognized a solution. The woman stepped into the street.

A voice swirling, yelled, "Get out of the way!" but it was too late. Hooves pounded and then penetrated her chest. The last thing she heard was a voice protesting, "I didn't see her! She walked right into the street. I couldn't stop. She walked into the street like she didn't see a thing. I couldn't help it."

Her body was kneaded by horses' hooves like she was a loaf of bread in the making. One hoof burrowed into the woman's soft abdomen, another into her tired brain before she was cast into the darkness of a warm oven. Red-light heat warmed her flesh, and she was no longer hungry, no longer cold. She felt nothing—no fear, no anger, no defeat, not even pain. There was only the sound of her thoughts whispering above the bitter wind: *In a small room on the fifth floor, a little boy waits…waits for me. I am not coming…I am not coming home. I don't have any bread. I have been battered and pounded and shaped. Feed me now to the horses and angels. There is nothing…nothing left.*

But I hurry, hurry, always hurrying, trying to get back to you, my son, as I promised. Somehow, someway I will bring you food.

* * * * *

"Mommy, Mommy."

I woke with a start. Mitchell, my six-year-old, stood by the couch in his turquoise snowsuit.

"We want to come in. Are we going to eat soon?"

"Oh, yes, yes. I'll make us something for lunch." I struggled for more reality, then remembered. It was Saturday morning. The children had gone outside to make a snowman with their father. "Did you make a snowman?" I asked.

"No, we made a snow rabbit. We were going to make a snowman, but we made a snow rabbit instead."

"A snow rabbit. Great idea."

I stared into the face of my sweet young son, who seemed perplexed. He wasn't accustomed to finding me on the sofa. "Do you need to go to the bathroom?" I asked, guessing the main reason he had come inside.

He nodded.

* * * * *

I decided to talk to my husband.

"There is something I…something I want us to talk about," I said. The children were asleep, and we sat down at the kitchen table. I poured a cup of tea for myself. John didn't want any.

"I had a dream. It was so real I think it might be a past lifetime. I dreamed…I dreamed I died."

I told John about how the article in the paper describing the death of Ozzie Bernhardt had affected me. He knew about the accident, had even been to see the psychiatrist who refused to treat him as long as his drinking continued. John listened to me quietly without a word. I knew I was taking a risk as great as the one the woman who went to beg the boy's father for food, and one equally necessary. I looked at John carefully, across the kitchen table, across time, searching to see if I could find that hungry little boy who waited for me. John looked at me painfully, and for a brief moment, the separation diminished.

I continued, "The woman is very sorry she did not come back. Please understand how sorry she is. Yes, it was an accident, but in another way, it was what she chose. It was wrong." I looked at him, but could not tell if he understood what I was saying. I reached for his hands resting on the table. I ached for forgiveness. I wanted a better life for us and our children.

"I am sorry," I said, almost whispering.

Whether or not he understood, he looked at me in abrupt coldness, or it could have been manipulation.

"You're sorry," he said and withdrew his hands. "How do you think that little boy felt?"

I had no answer.

*****

As a result of this and other experiences, I believe there is some validity in the concept of reincarnation. Remembrances of "past lives" do occur. However, reincarnation is not a matter of merely changing roles in subsequent lifetimes. Each life is completely unique. Life is meant for living in the present; focusing on past lives can be counterproductive. This particular "cellular memory" and other such memories helped me understand the dynamics of my first marriage—our attraction for one another, his addictive relationship to me, my feelings of guilt and need to take on too much responsibility, his wanting me not to work or go places alone, my desire to "take care" of him. Remembering this past time, if that's what it was, did not solve our problems. We were different people from the individuals in the dream and had contemporary issues. When I confronted John with what I believed might be the root of our difficulties, he quickly ended what might have been a new beginning for us. He was not going to provide what I felt I needed: forgiveness. Would I need to leave him again?

As for Ozzie, I don't know if they ever located the driver who had killed him. Was it an accident or had Ozzie subconsciously also looked for an escape because of difficulties he faced? I don't know. Is there any such thing as an accident? Can't a person simply be in the wrong place at the wrong time? Perhaps. But there are also knee-jerk accidents, thoughtless solutions that in the long term are not solutions at all.

14

Bedstefar Jens

In 1972, I took on the responsibility of overseeing the care for my *Bedstefar* ("Best or grand"-father, pronounced Best-uh-faa) who was in the Masonic Nursing Home, visiting him at least once a week, usually on Sunday, sometimes taking the children with me. My mother was caring for my grandmother, who was recovering from surgery, and she and my uncle, who lived in another state, found it heartbreaking to visit Bedstefar in his demented state.

After more than sixty years of marriage, my grandparents had to be separated. At the time, his illness was called "hardening of the arteries"; undoubtedly, it was Alzheimer's disease. Due to his dementia, Jens Juhl, a 32nd degree Mason, came to the Masonic home near my home in Iowa.

I always looked forward to our visiting my grandfather even though Bedstefar's brains seemed to have become oatmeal. When I went to see him, I totally relaxed. His disease provided me with a curious and soothing legacy. We could not communicate in the usual way; we had to reach across cognitive barriers to be with each other.

At the time I was working for United Way as Director of Government Relations in the Quad Cities, a bistate, bifederal, multilocal government area. Concerns about my family, my husband, my job, went away when Bedstefar and I sat together in his small room. Seeing Bedstefar became a highlight of my week, an Alice-in-Wonderland adventure, a time I could leave the demands of reality and enter my grandfather's world. Down the rabbit hole I would go, leaving the pulls of a stressful job, the needs of my young children, the negotiations of a difficult marriage and enter Jens Juhl's king-of-hearts nursing home room reality.

Often Bedstefar and I would sit for an hour, a kind of senile "Nordic-Buddhism sit." He would sometimes know me, but usually not. At times he would talk about the plumbing; the sink in his room really annoyed him.

Once when Bedstefar was sick with a fever, I was called to the nursing home. When I arrived, he was in bed, and to my amazement, he seemed to know who I was and who he was. He turned his head toward the wall, as if he didn't want me to see the only Bedstefar tear I ever saw roll down his ancient cheek.

I reached over and held his hand. "You are a good man, Bedstefar." I meant it with all my heart. I thought he would have died right then, but he lived on, and I wondered if he would live as long as there are Sundays.

*****

In the Great Depression, Jens Juhl had lost his managerial position in a lumberyard and became a janitor in the Clinton, Iowa, school system. As youngsters, we children loved to go to Bedstefar's school. It never occurred to us that it belonged to anyone but Bedstefar. He had all those keys dangling from his belt.

As children, we would walk through the cinder alley to meet him when he came home, sometime even in bare feet walking gingerly on the cinders. On our annual summer adventure to Clinton, Bedstefar would take us to the top floor of the old Kirkwood School, unlock the fire escape, a tunnel-slide that descended four stories! We would bravely plunk our little rears down inside the culvert-like metal tubing and in a born-again experience, slide down all four flights, our short legs stretched out to steer the way. No amusement park ride ever matched the thrill and magic of our birthright, the Kirkwood School's fire escape tube slide. Bedstefar had the keys to life's greatest experience. I was very proud of him.

"Can we do it again, Bedstefar? Can we do it again?" Yes, of course, we could do it again.

Discards from his Kirkwood school were a cornerstone of my early education. I especially loved the manila cards with words printed on them, stacks and stacks of 4" × 8" cards. Single words magically became ideas that meant something capable of being rearranged to mean something else entirely. Perhaps if those discarded cards had been numbers instead of words, I would have become a mathematician or an accountant.

When I was seven years old, the Kirkwood music teacher tossed out old elementary school band uniforms: red capes with red-and-black hats similar to the costume worn by Curious George, the storybook monkey. I received one of those classic uniforms from my Bedstefar—a red shiny cape that billowed behind me in the wind and the black-and-red pillbox held in place by a black strap under my chin. I loved that cape. If I started from the very top of a hill and ran very fast in my takeoff, I could fly. I was Mary Marvel.

Down the hill came Mary Marvel, crime fighter, all the way down the hill, my cape and I carried on the air, moments of glory, until at the bottom, where I was forced to become my ordinary self again.

Bedstefar had his own special territory in my grandparents' home—the basement. My grandmother clearly ruled the upstairs, but Bedstefar ruled the basement with its dominating octopus furnace, serving as a central sculpture around which to roller skate. There was also a large printing press in a corner where Bedstefar printed stationery with our names or initials on them and personalized napkins for my grandmother and her friends. He was an expert calligrapher; his woodworking was elegant. In the early 1900s, Jens made a dollhouse for my mother, with two hundred real wood shingles, colonnades, a front porch, and a red glass window on the side. His woodworking included a miniature oak buffet for my mother, an exact replica of the one he made for my grandmother.

To their friends, my grandparents were known as a single unit—Jens and Marie—and were famous for their arguments, which were unsacred rituals. My favorite Jens-and-Marie argument was about which one of them had wanted to build their home on Third Street (more than fifty years previously) and who had wanted to build up on the bluff.

"We should have built on the bluff," Marie, my grandmother, would say wistfully as we drove down Bluff Road.

Jens didn't say anything. He knew what was coming.

"It is so beautiful up here, and the homes are so nice," Marie would add, and then sadly, "but you wanted to build on Third Street."

"No," Jens said. "No, I didn't. *You* wanted to build on Third Street."

"It was you, Jens. You insisted we build where the land was cheaper and the ground was level. I remember. We should have built on the bluff."

"I was the one who wanted to build on the bluff," Jens said, insistently, almost as if they could still do it. And so on and so on.

Subjects for other arguments centered on the who, when, how, and where of their history together—who remembered what correctly, who had decided what, *how* much it had cost, *when* something happened, *where* it happened, *who* was present, etc. All Jens-and-Marie arguments were civilized—contentious, spirited, annoying, but civilized, with a sense of fairness and good sportsmanship. There was no real rancor, resentment, or bitterness—distain perhaps, but no real rancor. But who knows for sure? I was a child.

*****

In their nineties, health problems separated the two. Marie's body had become very fragile, and she had a long recuperation in a nursing home following surgery. Jens's brain failed him. They could no longer argue. Jens needed specialized care.

Upon sufficiently regaining her health, Bedstemor, my grandmother, asked to see my grandfather. My mother dreaded such a visit. My grandfather's health had taken a deeper dive. He might not recognize her, and he might say or do outlandish things (like swat a nurse on her posterior). Time was running out; the two of them would not live forever. Bedstemor's wishes would be honored.

Mother and I had inadvertently chosen one of those cold Sunday afternoons during which people visit nursing homes because there is nothing much better to do. It was an obviously miserable Sunday afternoon when Mother brought my ninety-two-year-old grandmother to once more see her ninety-two-year-old husband suffering from dementia.

I went in first to prepare him for the visit. "Hello!" I greeted Bedstefar, attempting to stir up the stagnant atmosphere in his nursing home room and dispel the gloomy Pine Sol-covered smell of old body urine. My old Bedstefar was tied to his wheelchair. Leftover orange gelatin topped with a whimsical dab of whipped cream languished in his plate. Oddly, I wanted to eat it.

"Hello," he called back, mocking my cheerfulness. He began his demented singsong, which he would often do for hours. This time it was "Yankee Doddle."

"Dah de dah de dah de dah…" Jens had always been musical, and now in his senility, he sang, or rather chanted, all the old favorites, driving some of the other residents and staff nearly crazy.

"It's Joy," I said, taking off my coat, identifying myself.

He looked at me a moment. The remaining hairs on his bald head stood up like unkempt strands of grass blades on an otherwise barren lawn; Jens had been a dandy in his youth, and always meticulously groomed.

"It is not!" he snapped angrily.

I sat down on his bed and looked at my grandfather. "Well then," I said, "who am I?"

"Asta!" he said. Wasn't it obvious? Surely I should know that I was my mother.

"How old is Joy then?" I asked.

"Five…" he said, but with less certainty. Then gaining confidence in his assertion, "She's five!"

I felt sympathy for my grandfather. It must be disconcerting to have a giant five-year-old come bouncing in while you are trying to eat your Jell-O.

"This is a very special day," I said. I had hoped it would be one of his "good" days. "Marie and Asta are coming to visit you." By now he would have forgotten that I was Asta. "They will be here soon!"

"Ooh?" he inquired and then seemed disinterested. He began to sing again. Humoresque. "Dah de dah de dah de dah de dah de dah de dah."

This would likely be the last time my grandparents would see each other; we had tried to prepare my grandmother. "He may not know you," my mother had told Bedstemor, who simply had nodded. "He can be very confused, and sometimes he…he sometimes hits people. He doesn't know what he is doing all the time. Sometimes he can't speak."

Bedstemor nodded again.

What must it be like, I wondered, after all these years, after all those days of doing, all the arguments, disappointments, triumphs, heartaches, accomplishments, remodeling projects, picnics and parties, times together—after all the love, the children, the grandchildren, and now great-grandchildren, what must it be like to see each other and say goodbye?

The nurse came in, took away the gelatin, and smoothed Bedstefar's hair. "So you are going to have company, Jens. Your wife and daughter are coming to see you. You gotta look good!" She removed his bib.

189

Bedstefar's legs hung frail beneath the pajamas they had put on him. Still, somehow, my grandfather showed remnants of youthful handsomeness. Unaware of his shortcomings, he made no pretense that things were better than they were.

I heard them coming down the hallway—my mother pushing my grandmother's wheelchair. "I'll be right back," I said and went out to meet them. I bent down and kissed my grandmother. Bedstemor's kind face was surrounded by her naturally tight kinky white curls. She had her familiar brave look. My mother looked worried.

I returned to Bedstefar's room. "There is someone here to see you, Bedstefar," I said again. "Marie is here." I said, "and Mother."

"Mother's here?" he said. He often called his wife "Mother," and I realized I was confusing him. "Marie and Asta," I said. We have way too many Maries in our family. My grandmother was Jens's Marie, and there was also Soren's Marie, married to Jens's brother, and another Marie Rodholm married to my grandmother's brother, who also was named Soren, so there were two aunts named Soren's Marie. It was as if the Danes had access to only a few names.

Mother and Bedstemor came in the room. A table was placed in front of Bedstefar. My grandmother sat across from him in her wheelchair. Her sight was now almost gone due to macular degeneration, but she would not admit to blindness. She preferred to consider hers simply a vision problem.

What should we expect of those two? An argument perhaps, some tears maybe? Memories perhaps or everyday talk? My grandmother was known for her practicality.

What I witnessed I would have never believed possible.

Bedstemor looked at him, trying to make out his likeness through her deteriorating eyes. Finally in a soft, endearing, most loving voice, she spoke to him romantically, with quiet tenderness. "Hello, Jens, my darling, my dearest, how are you?"

He seemed to know who she was. "All right," he managed. He was speaking in words.

"Oh, that's just fine, my darling." She held his hands. "I am so glad you are feeling all right. It is wonderful to see you."

She reached toward him and touched his cheek; he stared at her blankly.

"Are they being good to you, my darling?" He seemed to have no idea whether or not they were, but he answered her by simply repeating her words.

"Good to me." He looked at her hands holding his, turning their joined hands a little to the left and then to the right, bringing them slightly together, slightly apart, as if there were something familiar, something he could almost reach to, perhaps understand.

"My darling," she said again. I had no idea she ever called him darling. "You have a nice place here."

"Too many sinks," he said. "I have to fix the sink." Jens looked over at the sink in his room where he was prone to fixating his brain.

"Oh?" she said, momentarily brought into his strange reality of sinks that needed fixing.

He began to singsong, "Dah dah dee dah de dah."

She brought both of his hands together. I began to hum along with him. My mother joined in a verse of humming Humoresque. Bedstefar smiled; Bedstemor grinned.

We sat quietly for several more moments, until Bedstemor finally let go of his hands. It had been a very short time, but it was time to go. I was eager for them to leave. From my previous visits with Bedstefar, I knew his good behavior could change quickly. I did not want my grandmother to experience his craziness.

"I have to go now, my love," she said.

"Goodbye," he said simply.

"Goodbye, Jens. Goodbye, my darling." Her voice was soft and quiet. Tears were streaming down my face, but my grandmother did not weep, nor did my mother.

* * * * *

My grandfather lived so long past what seemed "useful" that for a while, I thought his life would never end. One day at work, I got the final call. "Your grandfather is very ill. Can you come up to the home?"

"Of course," I said. But it wasn't going to be easy. I needed to leave work, go home first, find a sitter. This was not the first time they had called.

When I reached the nursing home, my grandfather was in bed. His face was nearly as white as the strands of hair that fell across his forehead. Age spots, some as large as pennies, dotted his face. I took his hand. I talked about my children, but he did not respond other than to touch my hand with slight pressure. I decided to be quiet and simply sit with him. I had called my mother before I left work, but my father and grandmother were also both very ill; she needed to stay with them.

Bedstefar was asleep, unaware of me. "He could go on for days," the nurse said. After a couple of hours, I went home. Because he had been so long in his dying, I did not expect him to die that day. However, I was home only long enough to pay the babysitter and start dinner when the nursing administrator called. Bedstefar had died only minutes after I had left. All ninety-two-plus years of him had stopped breathing; Bedstefar had gone.

If only I had stayed! I should have been there. Why had going home seemed so important? Jens Juhl should not have died alone. I drove through the rain to the nursing home. By now it was nearly nightfall.

The nurse in charge talked gently to me, as she must have done countless times to other families. She told me my grandfather had quietly drifted off, sounding as if Bedstefar were on a raft going down the Mississippi River, which he had lived by his entire life. Even the nursing home overlooked the great Mississippi. Drifting off was a thought I liked. The nurse gave me a box of his things, just one box of invaluable nonreusable stuff after a whole lifetime.

"We already called the funeral home," she said, adding, "Would you like to go in and see him? There is no hurry."

I nodded, because it seemed the right thing to do. Until that day, I had never sat alone with a dead body.

I went into the room. Bedstefar's eyes were closed. His cleaned-up lifeless body was lying in his bed. I sat down next to him. For a long time, I sat there, just as we had sat together all those precious months, with few brain thoughts. I knew then how much I would miss him, how much our visits had meant to me. I loved this man, whom I knew so well and did not know at all. My Bedstefar had given me words when I was a child. Now he had lived his life, died, and gone on. What had his life meant? I did not know how to arrange my stack of words to make a sentence, a meaning. I only remembered a man, my dear Bedstefar, who turned off all the electric lights as soon as a person left a room, who got up before daybreak, who fixed things, made things, fretted too much, who loved to watch dancing girls on television, who had lived in my grandmother's shadow, but who was very much a person in his own place and time.

I felt so blessed to have had the time these past months, which had become years, to get to know him in his senility. I had come to know Bedstefar beyond ordinary communication. He had given me something even more precious than words. Together we had learned to communicate beyond thoughts to another level. I had come to really love him, and even if he had lost his mind, he had loved me in a way like no other love I had known. When I was with my Bedstefar, I was not a granddaughter nor a mother, a worker nor a wife. I was not even a friend. It was human being to human being, spirit to spirit at another level, where brains leave off and spirit begins. I was extremely grateful.

And so I said goodbye to my grandfather, not realizing that my relationship with him was soon to develop even further.

Jens and Marie Juhl with Tiny

15

Miss Miller

Bedstefar's funeral was held the following Monday, thirty-some miles upstream on the
Mississippi, in Clinton where he was born and lived
for ninety-two years in the same precinct. By Tuesday
morning, I was back in everyday reality. Mitch, my
imaginative seven-year-old son, was having problems
in school. It was time for another teacher's conference
with Miss Miller. Mitch had been almost cherished
by his first grade teacher, but his second grade teacher
did not feel that way. Miss Miller was not favorably
impressed by his sometimes whimsical behavior. The
situation had become sufficiently serious for her to
request a conference with both parents.

It all began over confusion of his name, Lee
Mitchell Martin. His paternal family tradition was
to use the second name of a male child for everyday
use and reserve the first name (in this case, Lee) for
special occasions, like Sunday-go-to-meeting clothes.
We called him Mitch. When Mitch began second

grade, Miss Miller, who had prepared numerous school records with his name as "Lee," insisted on calling him by his first name. He kept writing his name as "Mitch," which she crossed out with red pencil and wrote "Lee" in big letters. I wrote her a note explaining that we called him Mitch, then talked to her about it on the telephone, but she remained firm. His name *was* Lee, wasn't it?

Early in the school year, my husband had accompanied me to an open house in hopes of resolving the situation. John could be rather intimidating. He had walked up to Miss Miller and looking down from his six-foot-six inch frame and in his deep bass voice, boomed, "I understand you stole my son's name."

She spluttered an explanation, but after that, he was Mitch.

I was concerned because Miss Miller's constant disapproval was affecting Mitch—and Lee! He had even taken to sucking nervously on his undershirt and sometimes didn't want to go to school. He frequently lost his assignments and papers, and what he brought home from school seemed incomplete.

"Be nice," I said to my husband, recalling what had happened at the open house. "Please."

"Maybe I should stay home?" he suggested.

"She wants us both there."

"I won't say a word," he said, but I didn't believe him.

A stern Miss Miller began our parent-teacher conference with the statement "Your son has a problem," reaching across what apparently was interpreted as our barriers of denial. I resented that Miss Miller had the look of one basking in the role of a messenger with bad news. Mitch had been an exemplary student in first grade. I was having difficulty not holding her responsible for his disappointing performance.

"Well, what exactly does he *do* that is the basis of his problem?" I asked. I had only heard generalities—messy, not working to his potential, etc. I wanted something concrete in order to resolve her issues.

"He listens to the other class," Miss Miller said as if presenting something very distasteful.

I nodded. I was sure Mitch did listen to the other class, if it were more interesting.

"His desk…is…despicable!"

"Can we see it?" I asked.

"Of course," Miss Miller said. She rose from behind her desk, and led us down to a midrow seat. I wondered why Mitch wasn't seated closer to the front if he was having so many problems.

"Here," she said, standing before his closed desk, which apparently held incriminating evidence. "Open it," she directed.

Mitch's habitually messy father obediently opened the desk lid.

Miss Miller gasped in horror. It was worse than she had anticipated.

"Oh my!" I said. Inside the desk, stuck between a disarray of penmanship and construction papers, pencils, and broken crayons, was a tennis shoe. Miss

Miller turned crimson, causing the freckles on her face to ripen. "I had no idea there was a *shoe* in here!"

John did not laugh, but his shoulders were shaking. His lack of concern further distressed an already upset Miss Miller. "I fail to see any humor in this," she said.

John simply looked puzzled.

I picked up Mitch's worn sneaker. "Where's the other one?"

Miss Miller shrugged helplessly. "I have no idea!"

"I'll take this one home," I said, picking up the tennis shoe. Miss Miller nodded.

What can we do now? I wondered. How could I show Miss Miller how talented, smart, and fun Mitch was? All she could see was a messy, uncooperative little boy.

"What exactly is his problem academically?" I asked when we returned to her desk, holding his shoe discreetly at my side.

"His handwriting is very poor. He wants to read all the time. He reads *everything*."

"Good," John, who could devour two books in one day, said. Miss Miller glared but did not respond.

I tried to give John a sign to lay off. In spite of our differences, we had to find a way to work with Miss Miller before the problems became worse. "Maybe it's a problem of his not being coordinated," I said, hoping to find a "handicap" that might help her accept him.

Miss Miller took a deep breath and straightened her small frame. "Uncoordinated? Hah! I know what children are like when they're uncoordinated! I have had considerable experience with that! He's *not* uncoordinated! When I taught in Clinton, I had a child who was very uncoordinated. Mitch is not lacking in coordination, a problem I can handle. Mitch simply…"

John gave her an exasperated look; I was afraid he might lose patience.

"Oh, did you teach in Clinton?" I interrupted. "What school?"

"Kirkwood School, but..."

"Oh really," I said. "My grandfather worked at Kirkwood for many years."

John gave me a questioning look, but Miss Miller also looked at me and seemed curious.

"He just died a few days ago," I explained, thinking she might have known him. Everyone liked my grandfather. "Jens Juhl?"

Miss Miller's freckles seemed to disappear, leaving her very pale. She stared at me as she opened her small mouth, softly repeating his name, "Jens Juhl?"

"Yes, the funeral was just…"

"Yesterday," she said in a whisper. Her eyes filled with tears. "Lee Mitch? Mitch is Mr. Juhl's grandson?"

"Great-grandson," I said.

She stood up from behind her desk, her hands trembling. "He was…he was like a father to me."

"We used to call Kirkwood, Bedstefar's school," I said. "Bedstefar means 'grandfather.'"

"I know…" she said, "He told me. He told me about you. He talked about all his grandchildren." She walked away from the desk and toward the school windows, as if to distance herself. Standing by the school windows, she looked out on the playground. None of us said anything.

"I don't believe this," John said, shaking his head.

Miss Miller turned back from the school window toward us. "It *was* your grandfather's school," she said emotionally. "After he left, it was never the same. Mr. Juhl would come into our classrooms every evening to wash the blackboards and ask how our days went. If we were feeling down, he would listen to us and sometimes give advice. Mostly he would just listen and make us laugh. He always had a way of making us feel better. Mr. Juhl loved to tease… and the school was beautiful. He had such pride in the school."

"Yes, he did," I agreed, remembering the slide in the old Kirkwood school, remembering his ring of keys. Bedstefar was Lord of the Rings.

"He often took us out for ice cream," Miss Miller said.

"He did?" John asked incredulously. Jens Juhl had a reputation of being tight with his money.

"I was there Saturday night for the wake," she said, "but I did not go to the funeral. I had to teach, of course."

"We were there Saturday afternoon with the children, but went home that evening."

"Mr. Juhl's grandson…great-grandson in my classroom! I can't believe it. How is your grandmother?"

"She's doing fine. They were married almost seventy years, but…it was expected."

I stood up, still holding the tennis shoe by my side. John was already heading toward the door. Our interview was obviously over.

"Miss Miller," I said, "I'll work with Mitch on his penmanship at home. I'll make sure he completes his assignments."

She looked at me carefully, curiously, perhaps searching for some semblance of my grandfather. Her look was kindly, gentle, her eyes unmistakably moist. She seemed to have forgotten our original problem.

"I have several pictures of your grandfather. I'd like to show them to you."

"Perhaps you can come for dinner," I offered.

"I'd love to," Miss Miller said.

"On a Sunday? How about the Sunday after this coming one? I'll see if my grandmother can come too—if she's feeling well enough."

Miss Miller nodded. "That would be delightful."

"One o'clock, then," I said. "You know where we live?"

She nodded.

"I don't believe it. I just don't believe it," John said, shaking his head as we left the school building.

"It doesn't matter," I replied. "Just be glad." I glanced at the playground. Bedstefar had helped

202

supervise children before school and at recess. He rang a bell, swinging it in his hand when it was time to come in for recess or for school to begin. I looked out where the children played. I had no doubt that my Bedstefar was present—on the playground ringing his bell. I felt it so strongly that I had to thank him.

Thank you, Bedstefar, I said to my grandfather, who was present in some other form or dimension, another state of being that I could sense but not comprehend. *Thank you!*

Jens Juhl had managed to come back and help a little boy, his great grandson. He had come to do a great big favor for us, and to help his friend, Miss Miller—listen to her, give her advice, just like he once did after washing the blackboards in her classroom. The whole event bore his unmistakable craftsmanship—excellence combined with a special playfulness, almost a teasing. How could he have done it, this old, old man whose brain didn't even know Miss Miller was Mitch's teacher, who could no longer communicate in words—Jens's brain had died long before he finally did. How had God, Jens, or some combination of forces and coincidences presented us with this precious gift of grace? I had no idea, and it didn't matter.

Mr. Juhl, as he was called at Kirkwood, was really good at helping teachers and little kids. It was only natural he would continue to do so in eternity.

* * * * *

Mitch was excited that his teacher was coming to have dinner with us. When the anticipated Sunday came, Miss Miller brought a set of 8 × 10 photos of herself with Jens and several other Kirkwood teachers. From the twelve-years-ago photograph, Miss Miller, Bedstefar, Bedstemor, and several other teachers all smiled at me. Bedstefar looked vibrant and handsome at age 80; I was shocked at what these difficult twelve years had done to him.

In one of the photos, Jens was holding a golden bell, his retirement gift, a bell just like the one he rang in the school yard, except it was gold plated and inscribed. I could see in the photo that Miss Miller and Jens Juhl had been very good friends. She was younger and happier. I sensed her loneliness now and ached for her concern for children.

For dinner, I made a typical Sunday Midwestern dinner of fried chicken and mashed potatoes, mixed vegetables, cake, and ice cream. In the presence of a school teacher, the kids were on their best behavior. In spite of her failing eyesight, Bedstemor remembered Miss Miller; the two laughed together as they shared Kirkwood memories.

Before Miss Miller left, Mitch did his John Wayne and James Cagney imitations, which she enjoyed. (I didn't tell her that Mitch had done them at Bedstefar's wake.) As she left, she thanked me for a delightful afternoon and said softly so Mitch would not hear, "You know, I see a lot of Mr. Juhl in Mitch. I think he has some of your grandfather's humor."

"Yes," I said. "I believe he does!"

16

Bedstemor Marie

"Every age is wonderful," my grandmother once said. "No matter how old you are, there are special qualities to enjoy—except for the nineties. I don't care much for the nineties." With her usual practical optimism, she added, "But that's only 10 percent of a lifetime."

Now, Marie Juhl, my bedstemor, was in the same Masonic nursing home where her husband had died two years earlier. The last two years had been difficult. She was no longer able to see because of macular degeneration, and she constantly suffered from stomach problems. Now she too was dying.

For days, my mother had been at her bedside, singing Danish songs that seemed to ease her mother's discomfort. Often, Bedstemor sang along in Danish, sometimes in English:

> That cause can never be lost nor
> stayed

Which takes the path of what God
has made,
And is not trusting in walls and
towers,
But slowly growing from seed to
flowers.[1]

I sang "There's No Grandmother Just Like
Mine," a Danish children's song that seemed to be
written for my grandmother, especially the verse
which begins: "She tells stories while she knits."

One evening, after singing and then sitting
quietly for a moment, my grandmother suddenly
began talking. "No one understands me," she said.
Mother and I were surprised to hear her speaking so
clearly. A complaint from her was rare. Bedstemor
believed complaining was a weakness due to a lack of
imagination.

"I can't make them understand! All we do is
wait. I've been waiting for hours! It should not take
this long!" she said and began tossing and turning,
constantly complaining about not being understood.

My mother asked her, "Do you know where you
are? Where are you?"

"Ellis Island," Bedstemor answered, as clear as
the early summer night air. Didn't everyone know
that she was on the island waiting for entrance into
the United States?

My grandmother had entered another reality,
reversed time to when, at age 16, she had immigrated
to the United States to join her brother Soren. The

cumbersome process on Ellis Island was similar to what was happening in this nursing home where she was waiting for entrance, for life-ending, waiting for a new life. It was taking way too long! Bedstemor was impatient—nothing could be done to accelerate the process for entering this "new country," where the language was unfamiliar and she had no control. Marie Juhl was again forced to endure lengthy processing and a great deal of confusion.

The Ellis Island scenario lasted until the next afternoon when shortly before I arrived expecting to relieve my mother, Bedstemor entered a new state of peace.

"The doctor said she had only twenty-four hours to live, maybe less," my mother said.

"They've said that before," I answered. Several years earlier, my grandmother had been in a coma for three weeks with a tangle of tubes going in and out of her body like a chemistry experiment. When she awoke, she told us, "Don't plan my funeral until I tell you."

This time, I knew it would be different. My unconquerable grandmother would die. How odd it seemed—so many years and now only hours left.

"I can stay here with her," I said. "You should rest." My mother had been there for several days and most of the night before. "The kids are in school. You should go to the house and lie down awhile. I can call you if something happens."

"I need to be here," my mother said. "I don't want to leave." My mother had always seemed to feel inadequate before her mother, something I never understood. She needed to stay with her now.

Suddenly, Bedstemor had a job to do. Her time had come. She raised her head and blew short little breaths. As weak as she was, she tried to raise herself up on her elbows to support her frail, now shriveled body. She struggled, bearing down on hips that could no longer handle much body weight. Grunting, she leaned back, exhausted. With her eyes closed, she cried out.

"What's wrong?" I asked "Shall I call the nurse?"

"Wait a few minutes," Mother said.

We waited. Ten minutes went by. Bedstemor was silent.

I looked around the narrow room in the nursing home, where my grandmother had come when discharged from the hospital after her last surgery. So few of Bedstemor's things—no knitting, no quilts in progress, no pictures, not anything personal. Just a sink, a couple of chairs, a bed. How unlike the retirement home where she had lived for twelve years—the Sarah Harding Home, a place where Marie Juhl was admired and cherished, where she had served on its board of directors. No, this was a strange, clean, and sterile island, a place to wait and wait and wait some more for heaven to open its gates.

Suddenly Bedstemor's eyes opened, and she made a long, low moaning sound. Bearing down, with many short breaths, her elbows up, she cried out again and began breathing rapidly.

"I'm calling the nurse," I said, and reached for the call button just as Father Michael, an Episcopal priest and good friend, stuck his blond head around the door.

"How is it going?" he asked in his Texas drawl.

"Father Michael! I'm glad you came! Mother, this is Father Michael."

"Hello," Mother greeted him.

Father Michael smiled and shook Mother's hand.

"Would you like a chair?" Mother asked.

"No. No," Father Michael said. "I can only stay a few minutes. I just thought I'd drop in."

"It is good of you to come," I said, knowing he was not just dropping in. "I really appreciate it." I had told him my grandmother was ill, but I did not expect him to visit.

All her life, Bedstemor had been a member of a Danish Lutheran church. She had served as president of her Ladies' Aid for forty years. Now as she lay dying, she was far away from her church friends. Most had already died. She was also quite a long distance from a clergyman who knew her. She had outlived them all.

Father Michael went over to Bedstemor and stood at the bed rail "What is your grandmother's name?"

"Marie Juhl."

He patted her hand gently. "Marie," he said. "I'm Father Michael."

She did not respond.

"They think she has only a few hours, maybe a day," I said.

"Would you like me to pray?"

My mother nodded.

He opened his prayer book and took a white stole out of the leather bag he had brought with him. Placing it around his neck, he began to read from his prayer book:

"Jesus Christ said, 'Come to me, all you who labor and are burdened, and I will give you rest.'"

Oh dear, I thought. *That's really going to make her think she's on Ellis Island.*

Father Michael continued, "We pray for Marie, that she may rest from her labors and enter into the light of God's eternal Sabbath rest."

My grandmother began a quiet moaning.

"Merciful Savior, we commend your servant, Marie."

She began to take harder, longer breaths. Raising her body, she immodestly thrashed away the covers, exposing her ancient legs. My mother hastily replaced the covers.

Michael stared at my grandmother, then returned to his prayer book. "Receive her into the arms of your mercy…"

She groaned.

"… into the blessed rest of everlasting peace…"
Her body twisted in discomfort.

Father Michael placed his hand on her forehead. Despite her writhing body, he maintained a priestly authority as if baptizing a protesting infant.

"…and into the glorious company of the saints in light."

He turned to us, this young priest, face red and sweaty, his blue eyes shiny. "My God, she's in labor," he said.

We nodded.

"Let us pray," he said. "Our Father, who art in heaven, hallowed be thy name…"

We continued to sit silently while Bedstemor gave birth to death, her body rising up and down but much more quietly. She bore down and made a soft, short birthing cry. Then gradually, Bedstemor's labor pains subsided.

Father Michael made the sign of the cross on her forehead, carefully folded his stole, and replaced his prayer book in his small valise. He turned to us. "That was fantastic," he said, grinned, and left.

We waited. Her travail complete, Bedstemor saw a light at the end of the end-of-life or birth canal. From her responses, which seemed to be recognition followed by greetings, it seemed that some dear family members visible only to her were welcoming her.

Mother and I sang one more hymn:

> O Land of Our King
> Where harvest embraces the flowery spring.
> Where all things worth having forever remain

Where nothing we miss but our
sorrow and pain.
All mankind is longing to find and
explore
Thy beautiful shore.[2]

Finally, when it seemed necessary, we called a
nurse, who came and immediately shooed us out of
the room. "It will only take a minute and I'll call you
back," the nurses said.

Mother and I found ourselves waiting in the
hallway, waiting, as if we were now the immigrants
on Ellis Islands, people who did not know what to
do, who did not speak the language of the authorities. Should we open the door? Return to the room?
What was happening? What was the nurse doing?

A few moments passed before the door opened
and closed. The nurse stepped outside. "I'm very
sorry," she said. "She's gone."

"Oh no!" I gasped. Why had the nurses asked us
to leave? "We were just…just there." After waiting so
long, we had missed the ending.

"It often happens this way," the nurse said, trying to reassure us. "I don't know why. It seems like it
is easier to go when family are not in the room."

I put my arms around my mother. There was
nothing to say now.

It would be useless to protest.

"You can go back in now. Stay as long as you
like." While that was of no comfort whatsoever, we
did go back in to say goodbye. But Bedstemor had

already left, born herself into a new existence. She had entered the new country.

*****

My Bedstemor, Marie Juhl, left a lasting imprint on my life. She was born into a society where she did not blossom as noticeably as women do today. Her brother, Soren Rodholm, became president of Grand View College (now University), Dean of the Seminary, and with his great poetic gift, translated many of the songs and hymns I love the most. Marie expressed her talents as grandmother, mother, wife, cook, quilt-maker, knitting-teacher, volunteer, president of the Ladies' Aid, and board member of the YWCA as well as the Sara Harding home. She read widely. Her wisdom and practicality were legendary.

My grandmother's financial advice to me was something I often remember: "Don't go downtown into the stores; if you do, you'll find all kinds of things you need, things you never knew you needed." Then she added, "But if you do go downtown, keep your hands in your pockets."

I, along with her other grandchildren, nieces and nephews, friends' and neighbors' children were all beneficiaries of huge quantities of Bedstemor's unconditional love. She was our ombudsman, always on our side, finding ways to advance our causes, or comfort us—whether it meant a freshly baked cookie, money from the coffee can she hid on the top shelf in the kitchen cupboard, or believing in our future.

Marie Juhl knew how to cut right to the heart of the matter. When Kirsten, my sister's first baby, was born with Down syndrome, my mother was reluctant to give her the bad news. When my mother told her about the baby's problems, Bedstemor quickly responded with an emphatic, "So what?" Not that she did not understand the baby's condition. Her response quickly and firmly rejected pity in order to welcome Kirsten into our family with outstretched love.

When I was in college, Bedstemor said she was concerned about what would be lost when women no longer helped the community through volunteer work. Marie was given a medal from the King of Denmark for her volunteer work during World War II. She took great pride in the fact that she never worked for money; her work efforts had purity. I, however, needed the Women's Liberation movement.

My grandmother's most important legacy was her incredibly boundless capacity to love, accept, support, and believe in her grandchildren, as well as other children who had earned a similar role in her life. Bedstemor's inestimable love and support gave me strength more than once, and I plan to pass it on.

Marie Juhl in her nineties

17

Roxanne

The atmosphere in the Rock Island City Council was electric. More than two hundred angry citizens from the low-income west side of Rock Island jammed the council chambers. In addition to the residents, there were also community leaders, clergy, a few business leaders, and several reporters. I stood in the back with John, wondering what would happen.

An obese woman with a big heart and a long knife scar on her right arm was speaking to the council. "You have no right taking money from Project Now! They been here long before Model Cities, and they are doing a good job. They got me a job and helped get our kids in day care. When we need help, they be there!"

The place erupted into cheers and applause. "You tell 'em, Sammy!"

I liked my job as chief planner of Rock Island Model Cities. The five-million, five-year "War on Poverty" program attempted to eradicate poverty in Rock Island's poor neighborhood through comprehensive services that were planned by people in the community in partnership with the city; it was financed through Housing and Urban Development. Although it now seems ridiculous to end poverty in a matter of a few years, we were optimistic then. The first two years of the five year plan had gone well. New programs (including job training, housing services, health and mental health services, day care, legal aid and educational aids in the schools) had been established and were going well. But now there was trouble.

The next speaker was one of the few black high school teachers in Rock Island, Mrs. Johnson: "I'd like to speak on behalf of Project Now. You know I don't always agree with Vince [the director of Project Now], but the plan we put together in a whole lot of meetings included them, and it is not right for you to take them out. Why are you doing that? That is what I want to know. What is the real reason?"

I was curious how the mayor would answer. The rumor was that eliminating funds from Project Now was due to the agency's activities in opposing housing discrimination.

The somewhat pudgy mayor leaned forward. "Mrs. Johnson, I consider you a reasonable person."

The audience jeered.

"You must realize that we are eliminating considerably less than $50,000 from that organization's budget. Project Now does outreach services. You people should know by now what services are available."

"*You people.*" Now everyone was booing the mayor.

"I call for the vote," one of the councilmen said in an attempt to end the tension. It could get out of hand.

It was now or never. I walked to the front of the room. "I would be like to be recognized," I said.

The mayor hesitated a moment, then acknowledged me. "All right. What is it you have to say?" Because I was a city employee, he apparently thought I was going to defend the actions of the council.

"As chief planner, I am responsible for Model Cities' Third Year action plan. What you are voting on does not represent the plan which Model Cities residents and my staff developed. It eliminates positions of two Project Now outreach workers who were important to the success of Model Cities. The planning process has been violated. I no longer support this plan."

The room erupted into applause, with cheers loud enough that you could barely hear the vote being taken. The mayor gave me a look which was angry but perplexed. "All in favor? Opposed? (One negative vote.) This meeting is adjourned!"

Along with the rest of the crowd, John and I hurried down the stairs and out of the building as fast as we could. People were telling me what a good job I did, thanking me for speaking up. Someone even asked if I would run for congress. But I knew I had just lost my job.

Having lost credibility with city officials, I had to leave. I was vulnerable; I was an illegal. Model Cities was in Illinois. I lived in Iowa, across the river, which was overlooked until the next morning when I was called into the city manager's office and was asked to resign. During the weeks that followed, I believe my phone was tapped. I received a call from the ACLU offering their support should it be required. Before I left, I accompanied my boss, the Model Cities director, to Chicago and met with federal officials.

"Don't say one word, unless directly asked!" my boss Fred said. "Not one word!"

I agreed. There was no need. The city agreed to amend the plan to include Project Now. It was worth it to keep Model Cities.

Model Cities taught me there were places where I could not go. We all have such places, and it is interesting to find where the lines are. Project Now is an organization that has since continued and greatly expanded. It was not the last of my relationship with Project Now.

I had learned how to write grant proposals, a skill I truly enjoyed. It was better than writing novels. When I wrote a grant proposal (i.e., for a network of home day care services), once funded, I was able to see it materialize, visit it, meet the staff, see the children. Not a book, but real people! It was fantastic!

Soon I was offered a new position, jointly funded by the Bi-State United Way and the Scott County Iowa Office of Economic Opportunity to develop and fund priority programs in the bistate area. One of my first priorities was a bistate program to prevent and treat child abuse. For more than a year, all aspects of child abuse became my primary focus—working in two states, two federal regions, two court systems, and numerous governmental units. This included an experience I will not forget—accompanying a caseworker into a home where a baby had starved to death only two blocks away from the Model Cities health center, where medical and nutritional help was readily available. It was devastatingly un-understandable. The father had run to the fire station with his dying baby wrapped in a pink chenille bedspread. If I had not seen the body of this emaciated, starved child, I would not have believed it to be neglectful abuse. The parents had two other well-nourished children and were high school graduates. It was unforgivable, but the parents seemed overwhelmed rather than evil.

During the planning of an interstate child abuse prevention and treatment program, I met Roxanne. After our initial greetings, I said something I immediately regretted, "Your hair looks so nice."

"It's a wig," she responded quietly, her voice flat.

"It still looks nice," I managed, embarrassed. I had come to her office in the Bi-State Information and Referral office seeking her help in designing a comprehensive program to prevent and treat child abuse. Roxanne had the necessary data on what services were available. She also knew what was needed, and the differences then between the states of Illinois and Iowa in defining abuse, as well as state laws and treatment practices of child abuse cases. In my concentration on the new project, I had forgotten that Roxanne had breast cancer. It did not seem possible that this vibrant young woman, who seemed so healthy, could be seriously ill.

* * * * *

A year later Ed, my youthful boss at United Way, and I walked as quietly as possible down the aisle of a Unitarian Church looking around for accessible seats. Roxanne's funeral was already starting. We found two seats available in the center of a row halfway down the sanctuary. Fortunately, the people sitting in the pew moved over, and we were able to sit down quickly on the aisle.

I had assumed Roxanne would recover and was stunned when I first learned she died. Roxanne was far too young, too talented, and too good to die. We needed her. Roxanne was gifted—one of the exceptional people who helped others with a no-nonsense approach that was really helpful. Bright as a freshly minted copper penny and seemingly as durable, she was expected one day to become the director of the organization where she worked; it was not to be.

"We are here to celebrate Roxanne's life. It is appropriate," said the minister, "that her funeral is on a Friday. It was Roxanne's favorite day." He smiled. "Roxanne loved life. She loved her family, and she especially loved you, Larry and Steven. You were the center of her life, and she loved you dearly." I could only see the back of Roxanne's husband's stiffly held head, while the small boy's head beside him moved back and forth restlessly with the rest of his body.

"Roxanne loved life," the eulogist continued. "As you know, she loved the outdoors—hiking, camping, kayaking. Roxanne enjoyed music—all kinds of music from the Beatles to the Tri-State Symphony. She loved this community and gave generously of herself, perhaps too generously, in order to help others. More people than we will ever know have better lives because of the help she gave them.

"Let's listen to one of Roxanne's favorite songs about a special place she loved—San Francisco. Roxanne and Larry spent some very happy days there when they were first married."

Over the sound system of the glass-encased modern sanctuary, Tony Bennett began singing in his intense, casual style. The excellent sound system had such clarity it seemed as if Tony himself were present.

"I left my heart in San Francisco..." The melody spread out through the church, seeping through the windows and tumbling down the gentle, rolling Iowa suburban hillside so unlike San Francisco. We sat silently, listening, thinking about Roxanne and how unfair life can be!

The eulogist continued, "Yes, today is Friday. We will remember Roxanne on Fridays, on her favorite day. We will remember Roxanne when we are asked to lend a helping hand. Roxanne was an inspiration, a model for how to best help the less fortunate. Roxanne knew how to give help in a respectful way that strengthened and never crippled. What a rare gift! When we are confronted with someone needing help, we might well ask ourselves: what help would Roxanne give? Or withhold? What advice would she have for us? The help she gave so gracefully will continue to benefit hundreds of people, especially those who came to the Women's and Children's Shelter that Roxanne was instrumental in establishing. While Roxanne is no longer with us, what she has begun, her memory and her values will live on.

"We will not forget you, Roxanne. You live on in Steven, your beautiful son, and in the love of your life, Larry. We thank you, Roxanne, because we believe more in people because you believed in them. That is your legacy."

* * * * *

I was told Roxanne's husband did not want to cooperate with the usual obituary write-up for the newspaper and insisted on writing one entirely himself. Days passed with no obituary. When finally published, it was not much different than any other obituary. All Larry had managed to change was to insert a few tender words—"the loving beautiful wife, the magical mother of Steven." As in most obituaries, Roxanne's life, was reduced to the usual few paragraphs—her education, a short work history, names of family members whose deaths preceded hers, a list of survivors, the time and place of the funeral, where to send memorials, the who, what, when, and where. Not included was the intensely private *how* or the unknown *why*. Did she die quietly, passionately, painfully, contented, aware, conscious, frightened or faithful? No matter. She was simply gone.

* * * * *

My friend and boss, Ed, a Roman Catholic who once had thought of entering the priesthood, leaned over and whispered, "Let's hear it for the resurrection." I smiled. I liked the service, the tribute to Roxanne, but I too missed references to an afterlife, a new life waiting for Roxanne, like fresh clothes on a spring clothesline. The possibility would have been comforting. Tony's "San Francisco" was lovely, but I missed "Let us Gather at the River," or "Our Father has Light in his Window," "Going Home" or "Amazing Grace" I longed for tradition, ritual to soothe where ordinary songs and words fail.

"It is the wish of the family," the minister continued as the service concluded, "that we gather outside to celebrate Roxanne's life. Please join us for Cokes and refreshments on the lawn."

We stood silently as the immediate family left the church. Larry and little Steven were the first to go. Lawrence moved like a robot; he was not at all like I had expected from his passionate stand with the newspaper. Steven, their son, held a soft bunny—a velveteen rabbit—in one hand and his father's hand with the other.

"Life goes on," I heard someone say. "It's tough, but life goes on."

Although it was too cool outside, we drank our Coca-Colas and munched cheese and crackers. As a rule, Roxanne didn't like sweets, but she evidently liked chocolate chip cookies, because those were really good.

After a short walk through the crowd, Ed returned to where I stood waiting to leave. He brushed back his hair which, as usual lapped onto his forehead. "Want to go to Jimmy's?" he asked.

"You want to go to a bar?" I asked, surprised. I had assumed we'd return to work. Several hours remained in the workday.

"Frankly, yes."

"Okay," I said. "You're the boss."

The two of us completed a celebration of Roxanne's life at Jimmy's. Roxanne always liked a good margarita, so I had two of them. Perhaps she joined us.

* * * * *

Thirty years later, I was diagnosed with breast cancer. Fortunately, it was identified in the very early stages, but at the time, I truly thought I was going to die, that I would be one of the losers on that side of the statistics—strange, because prior to the biopsy and final diagnosis, I was certain I couldn't possibly have breast cancer. I was going to ignore the referral for a biopsy. I had planned a trip to California and often had call-backs for further tests following mammograms. It was only when a friend of many years confronted me with a severe "Get the damned test!" that I relented and quickly scheduled a biopsy, no small feat where I lived in the north woods. Even when I received the call from the doctor while in California, my first thought was, *What a nice doctor to go to all the trouble of calling me personally to say I don't have cancer.* At the time, my ego did not allow the possibility that I had cancer, but once I heard the words and fully confronted the data, I thought my life would be ending. I still think that was a very real possibility if things had gone differently. My mother underwent surgery for breast cancer when I was in college. I remembered my fear that she might die and the difficulty in confronting her illness then. Now it was repeating in my own body.

Amazing progress in the treatment of breast cancer has occurred in the last three decades. Many more powerful and complex drugs, along with their various side effects, have been developed. There is also digital and 3D mammography with earlier detection, more precise and safer radiation, less radical surgery, preventive education, and increased openness about the disease. Increased rates of survival are the result.

Alternative health also has made equally enormous strides— vitamin therapy, massage, breath work, diet, exercise, spiritual counseling, prayer, meditation, and mantras.

In view of the complexity of various regimens and alternatives, I did considerable research on the internet, read several books on healing as well as research studies, consulted chiropractor friends as well as a naturopath, nurse-practitioners, and talked to survivors. I wanted to integrate modern medicine with alternative treatment. The journey became nothing less than a restart in life.

In April 2008, I underwent a double lumpectomy, and in June that year, I had radiation treatment from within rather than outside the breasts (MammoSite). I declined chemo and drug therapy. I became more conscious of nutrition and began taking doses of Vitamin D3 and C. Because I discovered I was a shallow breather, I began doing breath work beginning with an intensive four-day retreat. Sufficient amounts of oxygen were not reaching my chest, and I learned to practice meditation and breathe more deeply. I sought new avenues of healing, working intensively with my chakras, reciting mantras, and also took up exercise. I tried to eat as much organic food as possible since the type of cancer I had is vulnerable to pesticides.

Please note this was the treatment I designed for me; it is not meant to be a general prescription for anyone else. Everyone needs to find her own way, using the best of help from modern and alternative medicine as well as chosen spiritual practice.

During my treatment year, I experienced deep pools of grief without knowing what they were about, and several healings in a variety of spiritual venues ranging from a Christian healing service and Buddhist teachings to Hindu mysticism.

One could say that I was lucky or that it was simply a matter of early detection. I have had no reoccurrence, which can be attributed to early identification and treatment, the medical model. Or perhaps, I woke up and realized my life required a new and deeper spirituality. I came to know–I am.

One of the mantras recommended to me early on, and which repeatedly got my attention was from Louise Hay's *You Can Heal Your Life.* Hay identifies the probable cause of breast problems as a refusal to nourish the self, putting everyone else first. The mantra she recommends is, *"I am important. I count. I now care for and nourish myself with love and with joy. I allow others the freedom to be who they are. We are all safe and free."*[1]

Louise got my attention. This may not be the entire story as to the cause of breast cancer. Everyone I know who has experienced breast cancer does not appear to neglect self, and vice versa, but the words resonated with me. I had also read a surprising study about women who had breast cancer. The results of the study showed that those who complained had the best survival rate. I've always been one who will say "everything is fine" no matter how I feel. I don't do that anymore.

Looking back, I wonder about Roxanne, her devotion to her work. Was her commitment to others so great that it became a detriment to her own health and life? Perhaps. Maybe or maybe not. What about my mother? Do similar personality traits create a propensity for certain illnesses? I really do not know, but my life became much richer for having confronted and handled what I believe was a primary cause of my breast cancer. I took greater charge of my life, paying more attention to my soul.

18

Father Gordon

On the evening of our wedding anniversary, June 10, 1974, I took a walk. It was a gorgeous sunny day. John, as usual, had forgotten our anniversary. He had not come home from work. Suddenly, without any reason, as I turned the corner around the block, I made a clear decision. This was not going to be my life. My name was Joy. I loved life, and I was going to enjoy it. I didn't know how, because I was still committed to my marriage and my family. But I knew one thing. I was going to have a good and happy life! Looking back, that was a momentous decision; everything else followed.

One Sunday at church, the bishop told a joke. "There was this man," said the Iowa bishop of the Episcopal Church, beginning his sermon with a joke while visiting St. Peter's Episcopal Church, "who was very difficult." I usually feel uneasy when a clergyman begins a sermon with a joke because often their jokes aren't very funny. The bishop proceeded, "Every morning when he came to breakfast, he would criticize his wife's cooking. When she prepared scrambled eggs, he would say he had wanted them sunny-side up. When she made them sunny-side up, he insisted he had wanted them over-easy. Nothing she could do ever pleased him.

"One morning, his wife, as usual, trying to please him, decided to fry one egg sunny-side up and fry the other one over easy, which she did and then waited eagerly for her husband to come down for breakfast. He took one look at his plate and then turned to her, complaining, "You fried the wrong one!"

Laughter spread throughout the congregation. I did not laugh. The bishop continued, "That woman was Christlike. She was patient, loving…"

And stupid! I thought. *Stupid!*

The remainder of the sermon had other examples of what it meant to be Christlike, but I was still too distressed over the bishop's joke to pay much attention. Afterward at coffee hour, while others crowded around the bishop, I complained to Gordon Roberts, the church priest and my friend.

"I didn't like that sermon," I said.

"What do you mean?"

"That joke. It was really stupid. The woman frying the wrong egg? That's not Christlike."

"It is kind of a dumb joke," he conceded, "but why does it upset you so much?"

I turned away from him and headed for the door. I wanted, but did not trust myself to tell him, "Father Gordon…that is the way my life is. I have been frying the wrong eggs for years. No matter what I do, it is wrong, and it is getting worse! I…I can't do it anymore! It has nothing to do with being Christlike."

Inadvertently, the bishop had brought me to the brink of a decision about my marriage. There would be no turning back.

A few weeks later at a healing service in the same Episcopal Church, I took my burden to the altar for a healing blessing. That night Father Gordon was assisted by Father McLaughlin, who bent to ask me, "What kind of healing are you asking for?"

"I want to know whether or not to divorce my husband," I answered. He stepped back. Father McLaughlin knew nothing of our marriage difficulties. He laid his hands on my head and prayed that I may be given discernment and make the best choice between two difficult paths. Discernment was exactly what I needed; I left the healing service strengthened.

* * * * *

More than a year earlier, John and I had tried what I had thought was our last chance. Gathering together all the money we had (alcohol treatment then was not covered by insurance) John went for a month-long treatment program in Hazelton, Minnesota, widely considered the best place in the country to treat alcohol addiction. I wanted him to have the best help possible.

Halfway through his thirty-day program, the children and I had visited him. It was a beautiful spring day, and it was as if we were a family again. John appeared to be free from whatever demon caused his drinking. He said he had found God while playing horseshoes, that he had "let go and let God." His counselor met with the two of us and said she thought we had a good chance. A good chance? Of course we had a good chance. I was filled with hope.

But when he returned home from Hazelton, life with John became nearly impossible. John's response to treatment was different from what anyone else's experience as far as I have ever been able to determine. While he no longer drank, his behavior became increasingly bizarre. John had quit his job as editor of the weekly suburban newspaper. We had purchased a used-books store, and I had established a consulting business over the bookstore to share the building rental. It seemed an ideal situation; the bookstore seemed like a perfect low-pressure job for him. He was extremely well read and knew a lot about books.

But John often would ignore customers waiting to purchase a book while he engaged in a lengthy conversation with a visitor. At the end of the day, he began to empty out the till and give all the money away, proclaiming that he lived twenty-four hours a day as recommended by Alcoholics Anonymous. His fixation about twenty-four hours grew worse— he would not allow any social commitments that occurred more than twenty-four hours in the future. When it came time to paying bills, he insisted we should no longer have electricity in the house. While a lamp or light fixture can be turned off, the electricity remained on. For me to handle my busy life, electricity was essential. John disagreed, saying that my wanting electricity meant I wanted him to drink. In desperation, I offered to move into the country and live somewhere without electricity, but he declined because of the bookstore. Whether or not to pay the electric bill became a high-noon standoff.

For John, alcohol was his self-medication, and when he stopped drinking, serious mental health problems emerged. I appealed to his friends in AA. John seemed fine to them, and his sponsor suggested that I didn't want my husband to be well.

"This is not well," I said.

As the months passed, I began having severe pain in my neck and shoulders. Before, when John drank, we had some good days, even good weeks. Now there were few, if any, good times. John had become extremely irritable. When we would go somewhere in the car, my having my head too far forward or too far back would cause him such upset that he would stop the car and turn around, returning home because of what I had done. I had fried the wrong egg yet again.

John went to Hazelton an agnostic; he returned sober with Bible and prayer book in hand. At first, I was grateful that he had found God and religion, which I thought would help him, but something was very wrong. One evening, he insisted that I sit on the sofa while he walked up and down the living room reading the Bible to me. As he preached, he became very intense and claimed I was the real alcoholic, but since I drank little, it was harder to cure me. His behavior was so strange that I no longer dared disagree with him. I looked into his eyes and could no longer see the man I had married. Years later, after John's death, I was told by a physician specializing in brain research, that children who have serious accidents often develop serious mental health problems as adults. John had been run over by a car as a child and had a steel plate in his head. Perhaps the basic problem was simply the result of a brain injury not properly handled. At any rate, I believe that divorcing John was the most loving and difficult act of my life.

* * * * *

In June 1978, I received a divorce in the morning and flew to Denmark in the afternoon. I was very nervous about my divorce. John had a habit of surprising me, showing up unannounced when I least expected him. He opposed my getting a divorce for irreconcilable differences, claiming we were not irreconcilable. I was being hypocritical since I could prove all of Iowa's legal causes for divorce, except irreconcilability. I was afraid he would show up in court and testify, insisting on a jury trial showing cause. My lawyer warned me that if he did so, I would not be able to leave the state. The house was sold, and I had accepted a job with United Way in Milwaukee. Thankfully John did not show up.

I had to get away. My health was beginning to suffer. I left my two sons on a farm with Iowa friends.

My daughter was with my sister and her husband in Hawaii on an archaeological dig. Due to blood pressure problems, my mother, who had also planned to come with me, was unable to travel. I went alone with my neck in a brace. For several weeks, I had been an early-morning outpatient with my head in traction at Osteopathic Hospital for "degenerating discs" in my neck, which they attempted to stretch—but the pain of treatment was more than I could tolerate. At home, I could not lie down, and spent most nights sleeping as best I could in a chair.

Somewhere over the Atlantic, I awoke. The plane was dark. For the first time in a long while, I was away from my children. The plane was only half full, and I was curled up on a couple of seats and had slept for several hours. On a movie screen a short distance from my seat, the young woman in the movie was crying out, "I have nothing! I have lost everything! Everything! What's going to happen to me?" She began to weep bitterly. I stared at the actress on the screen, identifying with her situation, whatever it was. Then quickly recovering from her emotional outburst, she looked up and said, "But I'm a good person. At least I have myself. Think what a mess I would be in if I weren't a good person!" She smiled, and her smile filled the dark airplane zooming toward Europe.

What a wake-up call! *She's right!* I thought. I too had myself; I was a good person. I wasn't alone; I had my kids and the support of friends and family. I would be moving to Milwaukee to a new job when I returned. Think what a mess I could be in if I were a bad person! Then I'd really have a challenge!

When I arrived in Denmark, I took off the neck brace and never had to wear it again. At the hospital, I had been told the damage to the discs in my neck was irreversible, but the problem never reoccurred.

In Denmark, I stayed with my uncle and aunt (my father's brother and sister) in Vjen, where I walked in the woods, rode my aunt's big iron bike to a nearby pond, watched the moon climb over the meadow each night, visited my Danish cousins, and slept in a feather bed—a very gentle countryside healing. Nothing was said or asked about my husband or divorce. At least, I don't think so—I speak only a little Danish.

In those two weeks, I became a young child again. Neither my aunt nor my uncle could speak English, and my Danish was limited to singing Danish songs with my uncle and speaking a two-year-old's vocabulary (my age when my parents stopped speaking Danish at home). When Ingeborg, my aunt, would tell me in Danish that I should go out and tell my uncle it was time for dinner, I knew exactly what she said. Beyond such adult-toddler exchanges, it was difficult, and we relied on Danish-American charades. When my cousin Martin came home from teaching in Greenland, he straightened out a number of misunderstandings. One of them had to do with the moon. My visit occurred a year following the astronauts' famous trip to the moon. As a volunteer, prior to my trip to Denmark, I had helped guard a piece of the moon at a local museum event.

One night looking at the moonlight over the meadow in Vjen, I tried to tell my aunt that I had seen a piece of the moon, a rock that was brought back by the astronauts, but Ingeborg had no idea what I was talking about in spite of our charades. Later she told Martin to let me know she had figured it out after she went to bed. But Ingeborg wanted me to know there were more fragments of the cross in Europe than could possibly have comprised the real cross. She doubted I really had seen a piece of the moon!

* * * * *

Two days after returning from Denmark, the truck came, and the children and I moved to Milwaukee. John had gone to a monastery for a couple of weeks. I no longer believed I could do anything that would help him. We both needed to go our separate ways. I am grateful to Alcoholics Anonymous, because I knew that his friends would watch over him.

John kept his promise as to what he would do if I divorced him—no support and no communication with us. I had hoped that my leaving would help him—that without me, he would get his life together, but it wasn't happening, at least not on my schedule, and I was terribly disappointed.

Apparently I had a low-level case of post-traumatic stress disorder. For years, there were times when I would see someone in the distance or out of the corner of my eye or hear a low familiar voice and think it was John; my hands would shake, and my chest would become tense. I was afraid he would suddenly show up in my office or at home. I also worried about him; he was ill. Once a year, I would make inquiries, take the kids, and go and find him. As difficult, disappointing, and even painful as these visits were, we needed to see him, but as tough as it was for the kids and me, John went through a worse hell for several years. He often went hungry; he lost enormous amounts of weight, grew a long beard for a while that made him nearly unrecognizable, got into gambling difficulties so serious he once had to leave town to avoid being beaten or worse.

Then, slowly, he seemed to get better.

* * * * *

For several months prior to leaving Iowa, I tried not to notice that Gordon, my priest and friend, occasionally stumbled on his way up the aisle of St. Peter's Episcopal Church. At first, it was barely noticeable. Anyone can have a problem moving feet over carpet. Then it became difficult for him to hold a chalice while he gave communion. Finally, he was diagnosed as having a rare illness, Shy-Drager Syndrome, a disease that progressively deteriorates the nervous system. Nerve cell after nerve cell becomes weaker, and muscle groups begin to fail—throat, diaphragm, sphincter, heart—dragging the body down in an agonizing drawn-out process.

By leaving the area, I had escaped the unpleasant aspects of Gordon's slow deterioration and with it the separation of a reluctant ill priest from his church; the sadness of his wife and children losing husband, father, and livelihood; the members of the congregation trying to meet conflicting needs of their priest, family, and church. What is the Christian thing to do when a congregation's priest is dying? The best you can.

I wanted very much to visit Gordon, but I was hundreds of miles away and was also afraid to see him. I was holding myself together and wanted him to be strong and healthy. But on a return trip to the Bettendorf Folk Festival in Iowa, the opportunity presented itself and was not to be ignored. Still in his fifties, Gordon was now helpless, weak, and unable to do anything for himself—but he was still alive and at home resting between recurrent hospital visits. He now needed constant care. Visiting would be difficult; Father Gordon could barely speak because of the severe weakness in his throat muscles.

My son Noah came with me along with my friend Rebecca, whom Father Gordon had baptized. Gordon had not flinched when I told him that Rebecca wanted to be baptized because she said her unborn baby had asked to be baptized. I was to be the baby's godmother.

"So you need to baptize the mother first," I explained.

"I'll be glad to talk with her," Father Gordon said.

"Rebecca wants a quiet ceremony. Her mother is a strict Unitarian, and she would be really upset."

"I understand." Father Gordon smiled.

It was a wonderful baptism—mother and child together. I stood up for both of them.

Now no longer living in the parsonage, Gordon and his family had moved to a smaller house. We knocked at the door, and Gordon's wife, Joyce, came to greet us. She was welcoming, but her usual enthusiasm for life was clearly waning.

"How is it going?" I asked.

"Hospice care isn't as rosy as you might think. It's hard. It's just plain hard. Gordon's upstairs," she added, indicating the way.

We climbed the stairs to the bedroom. In a corner, draped in a recliner, Gordon was half-sitting, half-leaning like a cloth doll. His shirt and trousers hung on him as if his body was a rack.

Each of us shook his hand, which was loosely connected to a wrist, which was loosely connected to his arm with so little muscle tone it could only respond passively. Nevertheless, we greeted him warmly, and in return Father Gordon made sounds, which we understood to be a greeting. He motioned us to sit down on nearby chairs. Now what? What do we say to a man who can't talk? What do we say to a priest who is dying, who has lost everything?

"You've written an article—or a book," I said to Gordon. "I hear Mary helped you with the manuscript."

241

He nodded and said something which I interpreted as praise for our mutual friend, Mary Shenk, who had taken difficult dictation, laboring with him for several months on a manuscript as he went about his dying work, relaying how his illness affected his faith journey.

I reported on folk festival activities, and Gordon nodded. We talked about a few of our friends, then about acquaintances and what they were doing. He smiled and tried to join in, struggling with great difficulty to say a few words, which we finally understood to include a pleasant expression about my ex-husband John and his new girlfriend. In spite of John's very difficult financial and emotional circumstances, he remained a fascinating, compelling man. It is humbling to know how easily one can be replaced.

As we talked, everything said became increasingly and wonderfully funny. We could understand very little of Gordon's speech, but in spite of it all, we understood *him!* Rebecca, Noah, and I looked at each other, gradually realizing Gordon was not at all pitiful. He was fantastic! His eyes had a merriment rarely seen or experienced!

Simultaneously in a distant place, but while altogether totally present, Father Gordon seemed to be looking at everything and everyone at once; it was as if he could see each of us individually and at the same time all humanity. As he tried to speak, we began to giggle, then laugh out loud. Gordon and Noah laughed. Rebecca and I laughed, entering into his contagious crazy world of wonder and pure joy, hopelessly joining in his revelry. From this incredible point of view, human foibles, including our own, were outrageously funny. The dying Gordon, from his external viewpoint of mankind, had a gracious, accepting enjoyment I had never before nor since experienced.

We wanted to stay. I didn't want to leave this dying-but-very-much-alive man who knew how to be here and at the same time in a higher state of profound hilarity. But finally, we laughed one more time and bade him goodbye.

What a great last time!

A few weeks later, I received a call that Gordon Roberts had died. Several months later, Gordon's article was published in an Episcopal journal, shorter than the version Mary had given me, the one Gordon had laboriously dictated, his visions or dream sequences eliminated. Perhaps some were delirious ramblings, but I was disappointed. Someone had edited out some truths.

In visiting Father Gordon that afternoon, we were given an unexpected view from outside this world—a peek at our continuing foibles, the on-going human comedy. With him we shared inconceivable bliss, acceptance, and outrageous merriment. Never shall I forget Father Gordon and that afternoon.

A glimpse of life *from* eternity. It's a very happy place.

19

Damian

By fall, after living for several months in the hotel Knickerbocker downtown, we were snug in a townhouse condo I had purchased in the northwest side of Milwaukee. The children were in school; I was getting settled into my new job. Gradually, we became friends with our neighbors, including a couple and their first baby, Damian, who lived in the next courtyard. I knew the father, Mike, who sang in the St. Paul's Episcopal Choir near the Knickerbocker, and who liked to compose. It was good to have someone with a common interest nearby.

But while I was slowly beginning to make new friends, I remained committed to my personal development. Every two weeks, I took the train to Chicago for a human development class with Gwen Osborn, whom I had met while in the quad cities. The purpose of the classes was to identify behavior patterns people wanted to change and to establish new goals in their lives. Gwen also led trips out of the country—to Russia, the Amazon, India, Hawaii. I hoped to go with the group as much as I could afford.

Returning home at midnight after a trip to Chicago attending one of Gwen's workshops, I unlocked the door and checked on the children, then tiredly walked into my bedroom, where I found a note on my bed.

It was from Thea. "Mike called," the note read. "Damian died tonight."

No, that isn't possible, I thought. *It can't be.*

I sat down on the edge of the bed holding the paper in my hand, unable to believe my daughter's note. Damian was not yet a year old. It was impossible. Mike and Fran must be heartbroken! Their condo in the next courtyard was filled to the brim with baby things. They were going through a rough time. A few weeks ago, Mike had lost his job. I had heard that Damian had the flu, but this was unbearable.

The next morning I went to see them. A bleary-eyed Mike answered the door.

"I'm so sorry," I said, "I had no idea Damian was that sick. I-I thought he just had the flu. I'm so sorry," I said again. "I-I had no idea."

"None of us did," said Mike quietly. Normally, he looked like he needed a shave, but this morning his bearded face was haunted, empty, dark. Fran sat silently in an overstuffed chair on the other side of the room looking out of the window. Her full maternal body stiffened when I went over to her.

"You were a wonderful mother to him," I said, hating the past tense. "I'm so sorry. You loved him so much, took such good care of him. I even thought you worried about him too much."

"Well, that was certainly disproved," said Fran, the irony shattering my efforts to comfort. How she had longed for a child. Now at only eleven months, when he was just learning to walk, Damian had died—after only a week of being ill. It was unbearable.

"I knew there was something wrong," Fran continued. She began to weep softly, making no effort to restrain the tears.. "Everyone said not to worry, but I knew…I knew from the start that he was really sick. No one believed me, but I knew. On Wednesday, he began projectile vomiting, and we took him to the hospital." She took a deep breath culminating in a sob. "He went into a downward spin. They still don't know why."

There was nothing to say. I sat on the floor beside her chair.

"He died from renal failure, but no one knows the reason. No one knows why! The doctors don't know!"

"I-I wish I had been here." I felt guilty for not being home.

Mike stretched his sleep deprived body, "When I came home," he said, "I couldn't sleep." He walked into the galley kitchen and stood over the sink. "I washed the dishes. His baby bottles were still in the sink. I washed them all." His back sagged as he stared at the bottles, upside down in the dish drain, bottles for no baby. For a moment, I wondered if Mike might start throwing things, but instead he turned back to us. "I wanted to take Damian to the funeral home myself," he said. "I wanted to take him from the hospital in the back of my car. We don't have the money! They just want to make money!" He banged his fist on the kitchen counter. "They wouldn't let me take my own son. Why couldn't I even do that?"

"I don't know," I answered. There were no answers, and there was no comfort. Mike was out of work, and now Damian had died. I was of no comfort. I wanted to go back home, but I stayed awhile, saying things that made no difference. Then I left.

The funeral would be Sunday afternoon at a mortuary. On that morning, I took the children to St Paul's Episcopal Church in downtown Milwaukee, where Damian had been baptized and my children went to Sunday school, where Mike and I both sang in the choir. After church, the Sunday school teachers had arranged for balloons to be released as a symbol of "letting go." It was an unbelievably fine September day—cool but sunny. Fall was on its way, but summer still reigned.

"I would like to keep some of the balloons for Damian," I said to a Sunday school teacher. "We can take them to the funeral home." My children looked at me doubtfully as I gathered a bouquet of blue, red, yellow, and green balloons filled with helium.

In the crisp blue morning, children, parents, and Sunday school teachers watched balloons rise rapidly into the sky and disappear. I turned to leave.

"Do you think we should bring balloons, Mom?" Thea asked, aware that they might be considered inappropriate at the funeral home, if not out-right embarrassing.

"Yes, I do. We need *something* to cheer us all up."

"Are you sure it will be okay?" Mitch asked.

"It will be fine."

"Damian liked balloons," Noah reasoned.

I forced the balloons into the back seat of our small white Mercury Lynx, squeezing my two sons between balloons.

"We can hardly move!"

"I can't see anything! This isn't going to work, Mom!"

"Don't worry," I said, but I was worried about my sight lines. "It isn't far!"

Before we were out of the church parking lot, Noah asked the tough question, "Why did Damian die?"

"I don't know. I just don't know. He had been very sick."

Bang! A balloon popped, and we all jumped.

"Are you really going to take these in the funeral home?" Thea asked.

"Yes, we really are."

It was a longer distance to the funeral home than estimated, but we made it with only two more burst balloons. When I got out of the car, I was less confident and tried to share the remaining balloons with each of the children, who refused my offer.

"No, you take them, Mom," my daughter said.

"All right," I agreed; it was my idea.

Seven or eight colored balloons in tow, we walked into the funeral home, my children a few steps safely behind me. The undertaker gave me a questioning look.

"We brought balloons for Damian," I said.

"We had them in church," Mitch explained, offering a token of legitimacy.

Thankfully, Mike saw us enter and came to greet us, taking the balloons. "I'm glad you brought them," Mike said. He looked surprisingly calm. "and I'm *really* glad to see you guys!" Mike took the balloons and walked up to the small white casket in the front of the room while we remained in the back. He placed the balloons next to a pedestal table, fastening them so they reached upward above a large bouquet of white chrysanthemums. He stood for a moment before the casket and then returned to where we stood waiting. "Thank you," he said. "Thanks, guys."

Slowly, the children and I walked up to the casket. We stood together looking at Damian's body. The child in the casket didn't seem at all like Damian. A baby boy, yes, but his face was puffed up and lifeless. He was gone…really gone. Fran came over to us and stood beside me. Her face was the color of gray stone.

"This is not hard for me," she said, and it almost sounded true. "That's not my son. What they have here is not Damian."

I nodded. The puffed body in the casket was completely unlike the little boy we knew and loved.

Other people were now streaming into the room. As we left the casket, I wanted to grab and hug each of my children, but I allowed them to go on ahead of me.

From the corner of my eyes, I saw a slight, sunken-looking old man, Damian's grandfather, the man for whom Damian had been named. "How's your father?" I asked Fran.

"'I have lived too long,'" Fran murmured in a monotone. "That's what he keeps saying: 'I have lived too long.'"

Mike handed me a small sheet of paper with a message from Mike, Fran, and Tonia, Mike's daughter by a previous marriage:

> He began his walk in this world,
> Yet his biggest step is to another life.
> Please carry Damian close to your heart.
> Now that his tears are gone, remember his smile.
> Once Love is born, it can never die.

Also on the sheet was the poem I had written as a way to work through my own grief.

"We had your poem printed up. Will you read it during the service? Jan Biggers did the sketch, and we copied it as best we could. We have so few photographs of Damian. Isn't it beautiful?"

I looked at the portrait by the mother of Mike's best friend.

"It is beautiful," I said, and agreed to read my poem:

Gifts of Damian

Hello there, Damian!
Long awaited child…
Loving and loved
Choosing you choosing us
Hello there, Damian!

You enlarged our days
Bringing to us new consciousness,
Teaching us life-secrets
(your baby body words
increased their meaning),
connecting the unconnectibles
while you played with your little toys.

You bonded us to deeper life.
Hello there, Damian!
For those who love and are loved
there is never enough time.
A thousand years is not enough time.
Hello there, Damian.

For those who love and are loved
there is no time.
There is no death. Dear Damian.

A few weeks passed before Thea went with me to see Fran and Mike. My sons did not want to go, but Thea agreed to come. We entered the living room, which had been loaded with baby gear: playpen, brightly colored blocks, toy cars, plastic trucks, big and smaller balls, soft plush animal toys, plastic key rings, teething rings, baby bottles, juice cups, baby swing, push toys, pound toys, and a rag "boy" doll. Now only a rocking chair remained as evidence of Damian days. I had never known a room so vacant.

We spoke awkwardly about the kids' schools, condominium happenings, but then I dared ask, "Have you done anything with Damian's ashes?"

Mike had told us they were going to distribute Damian's ashes in the woods beside the monastery at Holy Hill, a special place we liked to visit. Mike had wanted us to come with them. Perhaps he had gone ahead without us, wanting privacy.

"Not yet," he said. "We haven't gotten around to it. The ashes are in the cupboard. Want to see them?"

"No, that's not necessary," I replied. But Mike had already jumped up, gone to the hallway closet, and retrieved a small cardboard canister. "It looks like Ovaltine, doesn't it?" he said, handing the canister to my daughter. "Here."

Thea took them reluctantly.

"Shake them," Mike said, sternly. "You can hear little pieces of bone."

She stared at him. I didn't know what to do. Thea rattled the canister gently, dutifully, and quickly passed the canister to me.

Surely *this* was not Damian. "Shake it!" he said to me. I stared at him and then stared at the canister. I also shook it gently, obediently, and gave it back to Mike.

He stared at us, his eyes a bit wild, but he accepted the container of ashes back into his hands, and rattled it less gently than we had. "Do you hear the bone fragments?" he asked. We did not answer. Mike turned and walked away and placed Damian's ashes back in the cupboard.

"Mike, when you go to Holy Hill to distribute the ashes," I said, "let us know if you want us to come along."

Mike nodded, but we never heard any more about Damian's ashes.

Several months went by. Then one day Mike appeared at our back door looking even more haggard than the morning after Damian died. "Fran is leaving," he said. "It happens...it happens a lot when...when your child dies."

"Isn't there something you can do? Counseling?"

He shook his head. "No. We tried. Believe me, we tried."

"I'm sorry," I said. "I'm so sorry." There was little more either of us could say.

Time passed slowly. Then one morning, an early expectant spring day filled with the first warmth of promising sunshine, Fran came to see me. It was the first and only time she came to our townhouse. Surprised, I opened the door, but she didn't want to come inside.

"I came to say goodbye. We can't bear this together," she explained. "I need to make a life on my own." She stood on the patio outside and looked out over the green and sunny meadow beyond our condos, and so I joined her outdoors.

"I'm sorry, Fran. I wish it were different. If only it were different. But keep in touch with us. Let us know how you are."

Fran was about to leave, but then turned. There was something more she wanted to say. She added, "I had a wonderful dream," she said. "I dreamed my mother came back to see me. It was like...like she was inside Damian, that they were the same person, as if she came back through Damian but couldn't stay. She had to go again. But she, my mother, she comforted me."

"I'm glad!" I said, "I'm so glad." And I gave Fran a hug goodbye.

＊＊＊＊＊

For several weeks, we didn't see Mike. Then one day, Mike reappeared at our door. He came to tell us about the cause of the early ending of Damian's life.

"After all these months, they think it was measles. I kept hoping...hoping it was something rare. The doctors sent all kinds of tissue samples to the National Center of Disease Control. But all they could find were some *measles* inside him, measles that never popped out. If only…if only it were something else. If only it made sense—if only his death could mean they might find a cure for something. But measles!"

I didn't see what difference it made. Damian was gone. Fran was gone. Both were gone and were not coming back.

Mike had been looking down on the ground, but now he looked upward directly at me. He spoke bravely, "I'm leaving too," he said. "I'm…we lost the house," he said. "We had no health insurance." He shrugged by way of explanation. "I was insured under my old job, but it ran out before Damian died. They're taking the house."

"I'm so sorry!"

He sighed and tried to smile. "I do have a new job," Mike said.

"Well, that's good," I said.

"Yah," he said. "At least it's something."

* * * * *

If Damian had lived, he would be a man now, likely with children of his own. I'm sure he would have been very handsome and a very good person. Perhaps his lifetime was meant to be short, but such thoughts are influenced by hindsight.

Damian's gift to me was what I wrote in the poem: "For those who love and are loved, there is never enough time—a thousand years is not enough time. For those who love and are loved, there is no time, there is no death."

Damian Patrick Bricker
October 9, 1979–September 4, 1980

20

Israel

In February 1982, I found myself at the Wailing Wall in Jerusalem, listening to the heartfelt eerie wailing, wanting to scream! Here I was in Israel with my boyfriend on a tour only a month after beginning a new job at Mount Sinai Hospital in Chicago. My children were home with a babysitter; time off had been negotiated during my job interview. Stephan's father who was one of the tour leaders, and his mother was also on the tour.

Fellow travelers on the tour assumed Stephan and I were a couple; actually, we were about to go our separate ways. We knew our future was over (I was moving to another job in another state, and Stephen was eleven years younger than I), but we were not sufficiently brave to "cut off the tail of the cat quickly." Besides, we both wanted to go on this trip. Stephan was polite and distant.

I was sad, depressed, scared, and overwhelmed by the world around me, a perfect emotional storm—a dying romance, a new job, separated from my children, surrounded by a world of genocide, suicide, nasty politics, religious persecution, and the selling of cheap religious souvenirs. We had visited too many "maybe places" where Jesus maybe walked, raised Lazarus, or been crucified.

The Wailing Wall was a place I especially had looked forward to seeing because of my new job at Mount Sinai. It was to be a trip highlight. But before arriving at the Wall, Stephan and I had spent a day at the Holocaust Museum, the only ones in our tour group who wanted to go there. The tiny empty shoes in the Holocaust Museum that once held the feet of murdered babies and small children devastated me! What could possibly account for such inhumanity? Now, standing by the Wall, with its ironic proximity to the nearby mosque, my personal feelings of misery were exacerbated by Jerusalem's heavy, oppressive atmosphere of religious and cultural sorrow. I wanted to wail, wail, and wail for the lack of fulfillment I felt, for my expectant loneliness, for the centuries of pain and suffering in the name of religion. I wanted to join in the eerie wailing for the mass suicides at Masada, for border searching and bullet-ridden walls on the Golan Heights, for the stifling stench of old and new politics, and the constant selling of Christian religious trinkets by aggressive street vendors. But I dared not lament loudly because I was a Gentile; it seemed disrespectful. The others were mourning the loss of the temple, their ark. I was mourning life not being the way I wanted it.

As we walked through the narrow streets of old Jerusalem, the suffering of Christ, the destructiveness and suffering of people fighting to the death over this small land followed now by endless squabbling seemed more potent than Christ's resurrection. Distraught and downhearted would not do! I might never get back to Israel again. I girded my loins and managed to resemble a fascinated tourist.

Was there no escape? Peter had the right idea when he wanted to leave Jerusalem and go fishing. Like Peter, I longed for peace,

A few days later, by the Sea of Galilee, with its very deep clear blue water and surrounded by rolling green hills, I knew a quiet healing of my sorrowing spirit. As I gazed out from the hill believed to be the site of the Sermon on the Mount, I thought about the Beatitudes which Jesus had spoken: "Blessed are they who mourn for they shall be comforted." And I was comforted!

This world is not all pain, suffering, and nastiness. By the seaside in Galilee surrounded by the incredible beauty of creation, sea water renewed my strength, and a sense of peace rolled down the green-sloped hillside, wrapping me like swaddling clothes. The earth sang a lullaby.

In nature, there is communication with Mother Earth and reconciliation with God. When I looked out on Lake Superior from our Michigan home, I felt the same as I did that afternoon at the Sea of Galilee. When I was greeted by the vast rolling lake, with its incomparable gentleness, strength, and constant changes as well as continual presence, I was at peace and had some notion of what life is about. Now I feel much the same when I gaze at the mountains from my home in New Mexico. We are each part of a whole, and the whole is part of each one of us.

Life leads to endings. Endings lead to new life. Continuation and separation are two sides of one reality—a gift of creation itself.

21

Laura

Laura was my daughter Thea's best friend from the time they were second graders. She was the sister Thea never had, and they were very different. Laura's eyes were as sky blue as Thea's were deep earthen brown; Laura's flaxen blonde hair was as straight as Thea's cherry-chocolate hair was curly. From the time they were in second grade, the two girls were inseparable. They walked to school together every day; laughed and played together; often slept together; and went off to Brownies, the swimming pool, and softball games together. They were "me and Laura" and "me and Thea."

Their sturdy relationship flourished during the years we lived in Davenport, Iowa, a Tom Sawyer-Mississippi River kind of town, and followed our family to Milwaukee; they visited each other frequently in spite of the distance between them. Teenage soul sisters with dissimilar personalities, Laura was careful to eat vegetables and take lots of vitamins. Thea didn't worry that much about what she ate. Laura was cheerful and open; Thea was very private. Laura was a devout Catholic and sang in a popular religious singing group; Thea distrusted religion and often asked (with little success) to stay home on Sunday mornings when we went to church. (I eventually gave each of my three children the right to choose one Sunday each month to stay home. It worked wonders.)

Laura was an only child whose devoted parents' lives centered on her. Thea wrestled with the insecurity of being an adopted child and was only too glad to share her two brothers with Laura, who seemed like one of our family. The two also shared a sense of humor, expressed in mutual uncontrollable laughter.

Thea visited Laura in Davenport; Laura visited us in Milwaukee. The girls went off to college. When they became adult women, their lives began to go in different directions, but their love for each other never waned.

After I had moved my family to Oak Park, a Chicago suburb, Thea became seriously ill, culminating in a hospitalization with a dangerous infection. For several weeks, she was in Mount Sinai Hospital. We were warned her illness could reoccur. Thankfully, she recovered, and four years later, Thea had her own apartment, was working in a law firm, and I had moved to Evanston.

Late one night after going to bed, I received a call. Thea's voice was barely audible. Again, she was critically ill. An hour away, I knew there wasn't time for me to get to her; the infection required immediate attention. I told her to call 911. She whispered that she was unable to get out of bed and would be unable to open the door if help did arrive at her apartment.

Thea does not exaggerate her illnesses. I called 911 immediately and then telephoned my son who was staying in our Oak Park condo, closer to Thea.

Fireman broke through her second-story window into her apartment and brought her by ambulance to Mount Sinai. Thea had a massive internal infection. What followed were weeks of IVs, incredible pain, and finally emergency abdominal surgery. We brought her home, weak, depressed, angry, and still in pain. I telephoned Laura.

Now a nurse, Laura came to support, help, tease and comfort Thea, who was in a wheelchair. Once Laura arrived, the transformation was amazing. Within days, Laura's healing gifts had Thea out of the wheelchair and at the Lake Michigan beach, only four blocks from our Evanston condo. Soon the two young women were laughing again, teasing each other like the children they had once been. Thea was eating again; she began to gain weight. Laura had helped work a miracle.

✳✳✳✳✳

Two years later, midafternoon on a summer day, I received a phone call from a young woman, one of Laura's cousins. The news was so shocking that at first I could not comprehend it. I hung up the telephone. As I stumbled into the living room, I heard an unfamiliar wail—deeper, wider, and sharper but equally mournful to those at the Wailing Wall in Jerusalem. The wail was coming from inside of me.

After an hour or so of releasing my grief, I drove to the other side of the city to Thea's apartment. I could not tell her over the phone. I rang the bell; her boyfriend let me in. I told him what had happened and waited for Thea to come home from work.

When Thea saw me sitting in the living room of her loft apartment, she knew something awful had happened. "What's wrong?" she demanded.

"I would give *anything* to spare you the pain of what I must tell you," I said. "It's Laura."

"Laura? What about Laura?"

"It's…very …bad."

"What do you mean, it's very bad? Tell me!"

"They don't think she's going to make it."

"What? What's wrong with her?"

I took a deep breath to hold back my tears. "She tried to kill herself."

"Laura?"

"She's on life support. There's not…not much of a chance."

"I don't believe it. Laura wouldn't do that." Thea slowly sat down.

"She's in the hospital. St. Luke's. I don't know if we should go down there right away. If you want to, we will, but…there'll probably be a funeral in a few days, so you need to decide whether you can…want to…go…to both."

"Not Laura! No! No! Not Laura!" Thea was angry. "Of course I want to go. I want to go right now!"

I could not hold back tears any longer, but I had to tell her the worst part because I could not bear to tell her later. "She tried to hang herself."

"What!"

"She hanged herself…in her parents' basement."

"NO! She would not do that! She wouldn't! Not there! That's where we played. We played down there all the time!"

"Her mother found her when she went down to do the laundry. They cut her down, called the ambulance, but it was too late."

Now all of it had been said. The shock of the words hung in the air like…a hanging.

How can one comprehend the impossible when it happens to a precious loved one? Laura would never do anything like that, but she had. Laura was the strong one, the optimistic one, the healer, the lover of life, the one who always thought of others. What possible difficulty in life could cause a beloved only child, a Catholic, a beautiful young woman with her whole life before her to kill herself?

"Why? Just tell me why," Thea said, and now she was crying. Her boyfriend held her.

"No one knows. She didn't leave a note, but apparently she has been despondent."

"I hadn't heard from her for a long time," Thea said.

"We'll go in the morning, early. I'll pick you up about seven," I said, getting ready to leave. "We have a long drive."

"Can't we go now? Can't we go tonight?"

"It's best we wait until tomorrow. They don't expect a change."

* * * * *

We arrived at St Luke's Hospital before noon. Laura's mother and father were in the waiting room outside the ICU. Several aunts, uncles, and cousins were also gathered, occupying every chair. Some were crying; most sat quietly, looking miserable.

"This is the absolute worst day of all my life," Laura's mother said in a monotone, her face smooth, devoid of expression. "The worst day of my life," she repeated, as if having sustained the ultimate blow, it was strange to be alive.

Bert, Laura's father, a big teddy bear of a man who had protected his daughter all her life, who drove Laura a thousand miles to Milwaukee rather than have her fly or take a train, a father unable to protect his daughter from heartbreak or death, took refuge in caring for others. "You can go in and say good-bye whenever you want," he said gently. "We are going to wait another two hours. But her brain waves show that essentially she is gone."

What had happened to the miracle we had prayed for?

"We found on her driver's license that she wanted her organs donated. That is one of the reasons we are waiting. Do you want to go in?"

I nodded. Thea and I went in together.

Laura was lying in the hospital bed. An octopus of tubes invaded and engulfed her body. Her beautiful blonde hair lay limp around her face. A rope burn had scarred her neck, betraying what had happened. Laura's face was like her mother's, expressionless— no, Laura's face was lifeless.

Thea cried softly as we held our arms up, palms toward Laura to give a final blessing. "Blessings on your way, dear Laura. Blessings on your journey. We love you very much."

＊＊＊＊＊

Afterward, Thea and I walked toward the car in the parking lot, glancing down the familiar neighborhood streets. The hospital was less than three blocks from the home where we once lived when we had been a family of hope. Thea looked around, searching for the familiar. "This is where we played. We went through the hospital on our way to Sudlow [Junior High] when it was cold. They let us go from one entrance to another. They don't let you do that anymore."

We sat silently in the car for a few minutes, waiting for reality to shift from the too painful present, for life to become sufficiently normal to start the car. The sadness of a future without a Laura was more than we could fathom.

"That wasn't her. That was just her body. That wasn't her," Thea said. "I wish…I wish she had had a baby. Then there would be something left of her."

Nothing was left. How could someone so precious, whom we had loved so dearly, someone so close—leave us violently and unexpectedly, and we be no part of it, not be there for the parting?

Near sunset, Thea and I went to a concert down at the band shell on the Mississippi River front. The warm muggy air of the Mississippi added weight to the already too heavy goodbye. Sitting on hard wooden benches in front of the bandstand, I tried not to imagine what was happening in the hospital where a surgeon's hands would be reaching into Laura's body, taking out her organs—heart, liver, lungs, whatever they could use for other people who desperately wanted to live. Harvesting, they called it, as if her body were a ripened field.

"Whoever got Laura's organs is really lucky!" my son, Noah, said later. "I'll bet she had the healthiest organs anyone ever got!"

The inspirational upbeat singing group that previously had included Laura, began singing religious songs, some nostalgic and melodic, others peppy. They dedicated the concert to Laura, and featured a recording where Laura had a solo. The song was about how Jesus loved us, about our loving each other, and about how happy we all were. But at St Luke's Hospital, they were removing parts from Laura's body, and we were not happy.

* * * * *

What in God's name had happened? We learned later that Laura had been going to counseling, but the counselor would not or could not release information to her desperately wanting-to-understand family. Yes, there were boyfriend troubles and possibly despair from her work as a nurse in rehabilitation, which can be very discouraging, but nothing seemed to have the necessary depth of despair that could lead to suicide! Had reality betrayed her? Could it be that her world did not match the songs of being happy, loving Jesus and then making everyone else happy? Had something happened that we didn't know about? Had she done something that made her feel guilty? If only we could know. If only, if only, if only.

Three days later, we stood before Laura's casket at the funeral home—my children, Laura's sister and brothers and I, staring down at what seemed an unfamiliar body. "She doesn't look like Laura. She looks…she looks like Tammy Baker," my son Mitch said.

"And they probably have stuffing inside her," Noah, my youngest, added.

I cringed at the need for children to express painful truth. The undertaker asked me if we were family, and I said no, though I wanted to say yes.

"We were very good friends," I said.

"I have had several young people from that group," the undertaker told me. "I don't understand it…so many from the same singing group."

"From her singing group?"

"Yes. It's very strange. Five or six."

"Five or six deaths from the same group?"

"Yes. Young people. It's always hardest when they're so young."

Perhaps a coincidence or…or what? Despair? Accidents? Disease? I was going to ask. But he was already on the other side of the room. The service was about to start in the cathedral. I needed to go with my children.

Late that evening, Thea said, "I'm afraid Laura's done something…that's going to make it difficult for her, that she's gotten into trouble…done something which will make it really hard for her. Catholics aren't supposed to commit suicide."

I was surprised by her concern but understood. Are there consequences for choosing not to live out our lives, for suicide, especially if that is what we believe?

"We just don't know, but we know Laura was a wonderful person. And we know God is compassionate," I said.

* * * * *

A year or so later, Thea and I sat at the kitchen table with Laura's father and mother. I held a glass of ice tea in my hands. "I want to know what happened and why," her father said. I have put ads in the paper for months and months, asking people to come forward who knew what happened. I have heard from no one. Nothing. Someone has to know something about this!" Laura's mother simply shrugged.

I looked at the now childless couple. It was all so unmercifully sad. I wasn't hopeful. *The secret is locked inside Laura forever*, I thought. *We'll never know.*

"But I support my daughter," Bert said again. "If this is what she wanted, even if it was to die, I support her in it." Laura's mother turned away.

I wanted to reach across and take Bert's large powerful hands into mine. The house was empty, vacant of hope, unoccupied by a future, by grandchildren who would never be. Even Laura's cat had left the house.

After a few minutes, we thanked them for the ice tea, said our goodbyes, and went on our way.

My brief conversation with the undertaker still troubles me. Why would so many young people in an upbeat religious singing group die? It was not my business to find out, nor is it likely I would have learned anything. It would be cruel to raise questions for loving parents who finally had come to terms with the deaths of their children. It was a comment I did not have the right or the opportunity to pursue.

I think of a time when Thea was in preschool and I occasionally took her to the cathedral downtown for church, the beginning of Christian services with modern guitar music, which I enjoy. When I told her one morning that she and I were going downtown to the "big church," she looked at me and asked, "Is that the one where people pretend to love each other?"

I looked at her and realized she was right. It wasn't the music. It wasn't the guitars, but there was a falseness about that service, and a four-year old had set me straight. Perhaps it was just a matter of unfamiliarity. Going to churches where we pretend to love each other may be as harmful as going where we are threatened with hell and damnation. On the other hand, people may learn to love one another by at first pretending.

* * * * *

What about Laura? Are there consequences for murdering oneself? The act of suicide destroys the temples in which we live out our lives. People who commit suicide renounce and reject the critical life lessons awaiting them, lessons they have chosen and paid for dearly. They add to the difficulties of their souls' journeys, and they need our prayers. But I have faith in Laura and faith in God. When someone takes one's own life, the person is usually overwhelmed, distraught, not thinking straight. As Jesus said at his crucifixion, "They know not what they do."

If you should ever consider suicide, ask whether doing so might make things more difficult for yourself in the long run (spiritually speaking) as well as cause considerable pain for those left behind, often for generations. You can fall off your path for a while, take detours, stand still, and refuse to budge. You can kick dirt, walk backward, make U-turns, but you can't escape your path. We are part of God's intention for the universe; we are in this together.

In the end, the only resolution is surrender and acceptance.

Laura Taylor in junior high, 1978–1979

PART IV

*Acceptance,
Integration, and
New Beginnings*

22

Don and Joy

I had expected to move to the Chicago area in six months, so that my daughter could complete her senior year in high school. But June and graduation came and still no bids on the condo. Once we had passed the six months timetable, the stress of a challenging hundred-mile commute along with new home and job responsibilities became painful.

Oak Park was my suburb of choice, and I kept looking for a place I could afford. Then, one Friday afternoon in late June, I found an old thirteen-room Victorian house with four fireplaces. It needed a lot of work, but it was in an excellent location and had an apartment I could rent out. Reasonably priced, it seemed a dream come true, once all that "potential" was fixed up. My offer was immediately accepted, and I wrote a check for $1,000 earnest money. But the following Monday the realtor told me he had sold it to someone else and returned my check. What? We had a deal. He responded he got a better deal than mine, cash, and there was nothing I could do.

It was July; I had to do something and finally found a three-bedroom apartment on the outskirts of Oak Park. It seemed the best solution; the rent was low enough so that we could manage. But before the scheduled moving date, the landlord called to tell me I better find something else. He was in eviction proceedings with the current tenant, and there were problems—it could take many months, perhaps a year for court proceedings. He wished it were different, but I should find something else.

Now I was feeling desperate. School would be starting in a matter of weeks, and my family was still in Milwaukee. The commute was wearing me out. I went back to look at a condo I had seen earlier. It was more expensive than I wanted and small for our family, but I liked its charm and location. The developer, who specialized in converting historic apartment buildings, was having difficulty making sales in the stagnant market where interest rates now approached 17 percent. He asked me what it would take for me to buy it. I said, "You would have to buy my condo in Milwaukee."

To my amazement, he said. "Okay. How much? If it is as nice as you say, I'll do it."

In August 1982, I traded my Milwaukee condo for an Oak Park condo, plus a mortgage with variable interest. We moved before school began.

Situated in Oak Park's historic district, our new home had only two bedrooms, but was close to the downtown village and convenient to my job at Mount Sinai. Also, the schools were excellent. Hallelujah! We were settled and could reinvent our lives.

*****

"I have a game tonight," my son Mitch said early one Friday night the following spring, as we finished dinner. "You'll need to take me to the park."

"Okay. What time and where it is?" I asked, glad he was on the softball team.

"It's in Elmwood Park. I don't know the name of the park, but I can find it."

"And the time?"

"We're supposed to be there by six."

"Okay," I said, glancing at the clock. That gave me barely enough time to drop him off and make sure he had a ride home, before driving into the city. Thea was going out with friends, and Noah was going to a friend's birthday party.

"Better get ready," I said and quickly dressed for what was to be my first book-group meeting with a group of professional women on the near north side of Chicago. Invited by my new boss who was an ardent feminist, it promised to be a sophisticated evening. By staying up very late the night before, I had managed to finish rereading Jane Austin's *Pride and Prejudice.* There was nothing I enjoyed more than discussing a book. At 5:45, we climbed into the car. Mitch looked adorable in his uniform with his hat tilted sideways. He loved sports, and I was glad he was playing on a team.

"Okay. Tell me where to go." "

Sure, Mom."

We drove out of Oak Park and into Elmwood Park. At exactly six o'clock, we arrived at the ball field. No one was there.

"It must be in the other park," he said.

"Okay," I said. "Do you know where that is?"

"I think so."

And so we drove again. At the "other park," two other teams were lining up to play.

"Now what?"

"Well, maybe it is...well, there's one other place."

"One more try," I said, now impatient. There was no way I could get to the book club meeting in time. It was not only something I wanted to do, but my boss had invited me for the first time to the group, many of whom had recently been featured as Chicago's elite feminists. It would be interesting! Thankfully, Mitch finally had hit on the right location—back in Oak Park. I let him off. He ran to catch up with the coach. Fortunately, I saw someone who would take Mitch home.

Now I had the problem. I drove home to the apartment as quickly as I could to call my boss. It was after 6:30. If I were lucky, it would take me forty-five minutes to arrive at her home, but I could also expect parking problems. I telephoned her. "I'm going to be just a bit late. I should be there by 7:30. Is that all right?"

There was a pause on the other end of the line. To my surprise, she answered, "No, it isn't all right."

"Oh," I said, shocked. I had expected an "Of course. Thanks for calling." But there was only silence on the other end of the line.

"Well, okay. I'm sorry," I was about to explain what had happened, but decided to leave it alone. My boss had her priorities; finding ball parks for children was not one of them. "I'll see you Monday," I said, still hoping for a reprieve, but none came.

I hung up the telephone and stared at my paperback. Now who the hell would I talk to about Jane Austin?

Noah had already left for his friend's birthday party. I sat alone in the living room feeling abandoned. *This will not do*, I thought. *If I stay here tonight by myself, I will become depressed.*

Our condo was only a block away from Unity Temple, a Frank Lloyd Wright building. Once a month, they held a singles group, called The Discovery Group, which would be starting at 8:00. I had attended a few times, but was weary of singles groups. Frankly, it seemed like too much work, but what I did like about The Discovery Group was that most members were more interested in discovering how to live well as single people than finding their soul mates or someone to live with.

The group reflected the demographics of the Oak Park area, an odd mixture of ambitious young executives in their late twenties and thirties, delightful older widows in their early eighties, a couple of shaggy men in baggy pants who might be homeless, and everything in between. The programs centered around discussion topics, and while, unfortunately, it wasn't going to be Jane Austin's *Pride and Prejudice*, it would be something of interest. The discussion that evening turned out to be "The Importance of Friends," an easy topic, one that led to mindlessly easy, interesting tales and conversation from even the shyest participant. After the discussion, there was a table of refreshments.

Munching on some stale pretzels, I saw a pleasant-looking man across the room making his way toward me. Don Lenef introduced himself, saying he was an engineer, so I dutifully asked him about cars. I had dated two divorced engineers in previous months and had learned to talk about machines. "What's the best car?" I asked.

"A Toyota," he said and happily recited the advantages of Toyota automobiles.

"Is that what you drive?"

"No, I have a Honda."

"Oh," I said. "Why?"

I have forgotten his answer.

It turned out that Don lived less than two blocks away from our condo. He walked me home that evening and asked to see me the next evening. We saw each other three or four more evenings that week. Our first date occurred the coming weekend in Grant Park, listening to the Chicago Symphony under the stars. Both of us loved classical music and jazz. I could have asked him about Mozart or Charlie Parker.

Other than music, we seemed to have little in common. When we were college students, we would not have given each other a second glance, nor would we be considered a good match by any reputable cupid computer. Don is trained as an engineer; my interests and education are in the humanities. Don is Jewish; I am a Christian. He had never allowed a Christmas tree in his home; I celebrate Christmas as only a true Scandinavian can. Don is basically an indoor guy; I need to be outside—in nature. Don is a fix-it, linear thinker who loves technology and machines; machinery hates me. Don loves to cook and went into elaborate apologies when the first cake he made for me fell, while I stood speechless—battered by love, frosted with gratitude.

Our worlds are very different. Don insists he believes only in what he can see, touch, and feel, quite different from my view, but it depends on one's definition. From the first time he embraced me, I knew an unexpected, incredible world of goodness, strength, support, and love. This has never changed in our relationship.

What I didn't tell Don was that in fleeting moments, since coming to Oak Park, I had experienced glimpses of a man, someone whom I sensed lived close by, a very good person that I would meet. Meanwhile I had given up and attributed those experiences to wishful feelings. By the time I met Don, I had shoved the image completely aside from my consciousness.

After a year of constant dating, we bought a condo together and moved to Evanston.

On Thanksgiving weekend, 1987, we were married in the home of friends, where Don and I had often attended Gwen Osborn's human development classes. My mother accompanied the ceremony on the electronic organ. Don's son David and his fiancée sang a song I had composed as well as one David composed. Our friend Betty played "Jesu, Joy of Man Desiring" on her flute as each member of "the bridal party" (why not the "groom's party" or "the bride and groom's party?") walked down the aisle beginning with each of our children—Thea, Mitch, and Noah; and Don's sons: Alan and David. The large room was decorated with Hawaiian flowers—our work with Gwen included ancient Hawaiian spirituality. Our good friend, Pastor Max Kemling, performed the ceremony as his wife, Minnie, helped orchestrate the event. My sister and nieces all participated. David was in a dance band, and the entire band came and played following the reception. With food prepared by good friends, and well-wishing speeches, we danced and danced.

Our marriage vows included readings by my sister Karma, from first Corinthians, "*If I speak of men and of angels, but have not love, I am nothing,*" one from Gibran, and a Hebrew blessing:

> Barukh ha-or ba-olam.
> Barukh ha-or ba-olam.
> Barukh ha-or b'kalla ve khatan.

Radiant is the light of the world.
Radiant is the light of humanity.
Radiant is the light of the bride and
the bridegroom.

B'rookheem ha-khayim.
Blessed is life.

Blessed is the bond of love which has
brought you together and unites your
lives.

Representing our different heritages, the service included some of the Danish Lutheran service, the singing of the Lord's Prayer (which surprisingly had been a favorite of Don's father), and the wedding party drinking wine from a common cup with a Hebrew blessing. A Hawaiian blessing/lullaby was sung by those present "Ooh Lah, Cherished Ones, You are my Heart's Child. Happiness will come to you…All this World is Yours."

The surprise in our marriage is that we are much more of a united family than I would have predicted. Our children are closer to one another; and we are closer to each other's children and grandchildren than I had expected. Don has become "Danish by marriage," and I participate in Jewish services. Don still has some deep-seated prejudices toward Christianity, but for several years now, he served as Trout Creek Library's Santa Claus at Christmas, with excellent reviews (e.g., "the best Santa we ever had").

Our four sons have all married, and our daughters-in-law have enriched our lives, bringing their ethnic backgrounds and own spirituality to enrich our family. As for religion, it seems women in our family, as in most families, are the primary culture bearers. The religious backgrounds of our four daughters-in-law are Roman Catholic, Reformed Judaism (both parents were holocaust survivors), Greek Orthodox, and New Age. My daughter attends a nondenominational community church. We now have five beautiful grandchildren. While we are of different religions, we are one family. We don't need to change each other to experience community.

One could believe that my meeting Don that night was God's will. Perhaps that is true, but then a person might reason that God meant for Mitch to be unaware of where the park was and for my boss to refuse my request to come late to the book group. Maybe Jane Austin also had something to do with it; I would not have met Don if it hadn't been for her. If this be so, God or the Universe has incredible complicated schemes in which we participate—or mutually create.

Wondrous blessings are available to each of us through many opportunities, often in unexpected ways. Occasionally we have a glimpse, a fleeting moment of extraordinary sight, insight or outsight— and then forget about it until something or someone enters our lives and we recall that fleeting moment, that glimpse of another reality.

God's grace is always there, if we can only open ourselves to have and experience it.

November 27, 1987
Front Row: Noah Martin, Joy and Don, Thea Martin
Back Row; David Lenef, Mitch Martin, Alan Lenef

23

Max and Minnie

We called Max and Minnie the M&Ms. Like Don and I, they had contrasting personalities and interests. Max had grown up on a farm and was a Methodist minister. Before returning to serve churches in western Illinois and the Chicago area, Max had been a missionary in Mozambique. Minnie was a city girl who spent little time in church before meeting Max. In her prime, athletic Minnie in an Esther Williams bathing suit was perched proudly atop the shoulders of Dana Andrews–looking water skiers in the Wisconsin Dells/Tommy Bartlett water show. When she retired, Minnie was, hands down, the quickest worker on an early PC board assembly line. They were equally proud of past careers.

Max liked plain things—good soup and home-made bread. Minnie liked eating out and had a penchant for Louis XIV furniture and imitation gold leaf decor. Max remembered with some nostalgia when he found it shocking that a Christian woman would wear fancy perfume. But as a widowed grandfather, Max married Minnie, a woman who loved not only perfume but delighted in wearing low-cut blouses.

Max, unlike Minnie, never wanted or needed much money and was cautious about finances. Minnie loved money, treasured a bargain, and relished small luxuries. Max wore the same clothes year after year; Minnie dressed in the style of a much younger woman, with a fondness for high heels and sexy red boots.

Max had a beautiful garden where he nurtured tomatoes, zucchinis, and other vegetables. Minnie decorated ceramics.

Max loved to cook strange foods, like calf's tongue and cow brains; Minnie liked to eat out. Max liked to sit and talk. Minnie liked to dance and shop.

Max had an aversion to jewelry and found it difficult to appreciate and wear the large diamond ring Minnie gave him. Minnie owned a pirate's treasure of diamonds, rubies, sapphires and emeralds; she enjoyed wearing her jewels, even to hot summer picnics.

Max loved the Nebraska farm where he had grown up and was close to his six brothers; Minnie and the one sister whom she seldom saw had grown up in the Red River Valley.

Max's first wife, a nurse and close companion, served beside him in Mozambique, where they had lived in shacks and where she had borne several of their six children. Ruth had died instantly in a terrible automobile accident that occurred while Max was driving her home from work. He had seemed inconsolable. Minnie had buried two husbands, neither of which she seemed to miss all that much, but if Max talked about Ruth, Minnie would talk about Ken.

In short, Max and Minnie were exact opposites and made for each other. They fell deeply in love.

At their large church wedding in Itasca, Illinois, where Max was then the pastor, Minnie wore a magnificent long white gown. Max's frail mother and Minnie's frail father, as well as Max's energetic ringbearing grandchildren, took part in the ceremony. At the reception, Hawaiian dancers performed the hula on the lawn in front of the Methodist Church.

During the first year of their marriage, the M&Ms traveled in an RV all around the United States, which Minnie enjoyed, but Max longed for a home that didn't continually move around the country.

* * * * *

In August 1992, Don and I invited Max and Minnie to spend several days with us at our log cabin on Lake Superior. *These are my dear friends*, I thought as we enjoyed dinner together in front of the fireplace. These are the friends with whom I will grow old.

"Would you like us to bring your mother here to the cabin sometime?" Minnie asked as we washed dishes. "When we visit Max's brother in Nebraska, we could drive over to Grand Island and bring her back with us."

"That's way out of your way," I protested, "not to mention a very long trip up here."

"We'd be glad to do it," Minnie insisted. "I like your mother."

I thought about it. "Well, you could ask her if she would like to make the trip."

"I remember how she played the organ at your wedding," Minnie said.

"When we were kids, we would ask my Mom to 'Play with all your hands.' She would play in her jazzy style, and it sounded like she had six hands instead of two. My favorite was 'Red River Valley.' You should hear her play it."

"'Red River Valley!' That's my favorite song," Minnie said, and after a moment, "I want it sung at my funeral."

"Red River Valley?"

"Yes."

"You're kidding."

"No, I'm not," Minnie, slightly offended. "Think about the words…" Minnie began singing somewhat off key:

> From this valley they say you are leaving. I will miss your bright eyes and sweet smile…

Although I was unconvinced I decided to join her, and we sang together. The song evoked a memory from second grade in Kimballton, Iowa. The class had sung that song to me when we moved to South Dakota. I still think of it every time I hear that song.

> Come and sit by my side if you love
> me…
> Do not hasten to bid me adieu.
> But remember the Red River Valley!
> And the girl that has loved you so
> true!

"That's me!" Minnie said as we ended our duet. "I'm from the Red River Valley!"

A few days later, the four of us set off together on a trip across the Michigan Upper Peninsula to Mackinac Island. Minnie wanted to stay at the Grand Hotel, but the price seemed outrageous to our husbands, so we settled for lunch at the Grand Hotel and a walk on the veranda overlooking the grounds and Lake Huron, then checked into a pleasant-looking hotel near the marina.

At the desk, Minnie asked the clerk, "Do you have a safe?"

The clerk, a young woman, looked at her, mystified. "A safe?"

"For my jewelry," Minnie explained. "When I travel I always like to leave my jewelry in the hotel safe."

"No, ma'am. We don't have a safe," the clerk said, and looked at Minnie like she was out of her mind; Minnie didn't care. If the clerk didn't think

Minnie had valuable jewelry that deserved a safe, she was mistaken.

"I'll just have to do without," Minnie said.

We placed our luggage into our rooms, enjoying the island view and the breezy New England décor. Soon we were walking down the street looking into the shops. Minnie led the way to one of the many ice cream parlors.

I was first in line to give my order to a young man whose dark curly hair resembled chocolate swirls.

"Mackinac Island Fudge," I said.

"Single or double?"

"Single," I said.

"Mackinac Island Fudge," said Don. "Double."

"I'll have a double, too," echoed Max.

"What kind?"

"A double," Max repeated; his hearing aid had not picked up the question correctly.

"But what kind, sir?"

"Mackinaw Island Fudge."

"And you?"

"I'll have strawberry," Minnie said. "Four dips."

"You want a triple?" asked the clerk.

"No, I want four dips."

"Four?"

"She wants four dips." Max said, supporting his wife.

"You're getting *four* dips?" I asked. Minnie tended to count calories.

"It looks delicious!" Minnie said. "I love strawberry, and I always wanted a four dipper!"

The clerk gave her an astonished look, shrugged his shoulders and went to work. After a struggle of ice cream-balancing, he handed her a mammoth ice cream cone a foot tall. Smiling proudly, he cautioned, "Don't...don't let it tip!"

"I won't. I won't!" She took hold of the ice cream cone, her diamond and ruby rings flashing on four of her fingers.

"Minnie!" I gasped. "Can you eat all that?"

She nodded and began to lick the ice cream, her pink tongue making a path through a mountain range of rose-colored ice cream.

"That's the biggest ice cream cone I ever saw," Don said.

"Sure you can eat all that?" Max asked.

"I can eat it," she said.

Outside the village shops, we located a picnic table. Minnie ate all four dips of ice cream without difficulty. And the cone.

"Let's go for a bike ride!" Minnie said. Max and Minnie were adventurous poster seniors for healthy living. We agreed, and soon the four of us were lined up on rented bicycles for a trip around Mackinac Island. Sunlight splattered across our path as we pedaled single file, free as children on their first day of summer vacation; a whole world of innocence unfolded on the path before us. Gazing out at the storybook blue lake as we drove, we could see sailboats gliding on the intense blue water. The day could not have been more glorious.

Through the woods we rode. Alongside soft lapping waves of Lake Huron teasing the shoreline, we pedaled our bikes. The plan was to go partway around the seven-mile circumference of the island, but as we rode, it became apparent that biking around the entire island was within our reach and became our goal.

Everything went smoothly until the last eighth of a mile when the path became more strenuous and uphill and each of us experienced a sugar drop. When our hotel was finally in sight, we were glad.

As we dismounted from our bikes, Minnie uncharacteristically stumbled and fell to the ground. As if a stitch had been dropped in the universe, for a brief second, she looked terrified. A loose thread dangled from an otherwise perfect cosmic plan. Something extraordinary had occurred. "I don't understand what happened!" Minnie said. "I never do that." She struggled to her feet, trying to regain her confidence.

"Are you all right? Did you get hurt?" Max bent over her.

"No, I'm all right. I'm okay."

"Are you sure?" Max asked.

"I'm fine. I just...I don't understand what happened."

Something either had happened, or it only seemed so. Had Minnie simply lost her balance and fallen, or was something else occurring—a preparation, a kind of choosing in a moment out of time?

＊＊＊＊＊

Two weeks later, we met again, at Illinois' White Pines State Park for a wedding Max performed for our mutual friends, Larry and Cindy. They were married in a unique ceremony that combined the Methodist service, Hawaiian blessings and Native American customs. At the end, Max wrapped a blanket around the couple, signifying a new union.

"I have some great photographs from Mackinac Island," Minnie said as we left the wedding reception. "I had an extra set made for you." I was delighted, because we had not brought our camera on the trip. "But I forgot to bring them. Can you stop by our home?"

"Sure," I said, "but I need to check with our fellow passengers." To my disappointment, they were unwilling to stop by Max and Minnie's and see the photos.

"Let's just sit awhile," Minnie said. "I want to talk to you."

And so we sat together and talked a few minutes. I thought she had something important to tell me, but nothing important was said. There was strangeness, a reaching out, an unspoken incompleteness in our conversation; words could not match what we needed and wanted to say to each other because we did not know what it was. Perhaps it was simply because we could not stop and see the photographs.

More likely, it was that we wanted to say we loved each other.

*****

A month later, I was working late at my job at Swedish Covenant Hospital on last-minute details for the annual gala, when the volunteer chairperson telephoned to ask about the latest number of reservations. "I saw on the news," she began, "that a couple was killed in an automobile crash. I think they were on the guest list."

"Oh?'

"Yes, Kemling. I think the name was Kemling. I'm sure they were on the list. Weren't they friends of yours?"

"I…Kemling? Are you sure?"

"Oh, yes it's been all over the news. There was a terrible fiery crash. Burned to death. You should see the car. No one could survive something like that! I'm so sorry if they were your friends. I thought you knew."

"I…I have to go. I have to call home."

"We need to talk…"

"I'm sorry. I have to go…"

"But—"

"I…Goodbye." Shaking, I picked up the phone and called my husband. Surely it was not true. Not Max and Minnie. Gone. just like that? Burned to death?

"Yes, it is true," Don said. "I wanted to wait until you came home to tell you."

"What happened?

"A drunk driver. They were on their way home from an organ dedication at a church. A drunk woman hit them head on."

Oh God, I thought. Max's first wife had also been killed by a drunk driver. "I'm coming home."

The next morning, we obtained a copy of the *Daily Herald*. Below is the headline and photo caption from the October 24, 1992, issue:

> Couple Dies in Fiery Crash—
> Hoffman Estates,
> Woman, 37, Charged with
> Drunken Driving.

> Towing company representatives Friday look over the burned wreckage of a car in which two elderly people died as a result of a head-on collision late Thursday night.

They weren't elderly! Max was seventy-three and Minnie was sixty-six, but they were not elderly. They were young!

I went on to read the story:

> When Max Kemling's wife was killed by a drunk driver more than 15 years ago, the United Methodist minister was able to survive the loss

298

and continue working to help others through his religion…

…the crash occurred at about 10:10 p.m. in unincorporated Hanover Township, as the Kemlings were driving west on Golf Road in their gray 1987 Nissan station wagon. Schaumburg resident Lucy Stone of 2101 Hitching Post Lane was heading east on the road in a 1992 Chrevolet Blazer when she passed one car ahead of her and then drove into the back end of Hoffman Estates resident Michael Sassan's 1982 Nissan 280ZX.

The impact pushed Sassan's Nissan off the road, through a grassy area and into a nearby field. Stone then veered to the left into oncoming traffic, where she struck the Kemlings head-on at about 75 mph before spinning around and coming to a stop near the middle of the road, police said.

As a fire sparked and began spreading under the elderly couple's station wagon, about seven passing motorists struggled frantically to extricate the pair, who were unconscious and pinned inside the smashed car. But because of extensive damage to the car, rescue efforts were unsuccessful.

Authorities said they believed the woman was killed on impact and that the driver also may have died before the fire broke out. The Cook County Medical Examiner's office listed the couple's death as being the result of multiple injuries suffered in the incident.

Elgin firefighters later extinguished the car fire, but it took them more than 2 hours to extricate the two bodies from the station wagon, said Cook County Sheriff's Police spokeswoman Sally Daly.

* * * * *

The Mackinac Island photos were never found. Nor was any of Minnie's jewelry. Perhaps she had it with her in the car, or someone stole it entering their home following the accident. Unfortunately, the changes in their estate plans, which Minnie had discussed at the cabin, had not been completed, and so their estate was not handled according to their wishes.

As the visitation closed, double coffins paralleled the front of the little church where Max had been minister and where Minnie had been so proud of her husband. Don was with me at the wake. As he stood by their caskets that night, he had a strong sense of their presence. In spite of clinging to his logical, engineering ways, Don has had several "remarkable" experiences, which he usually finds ways to explain away. However, this was not one he rejected. Max and Minnie were present.

The funeral was held in a larger Methodist church in Elgin. Don was unable to attend the funeral because of work obligations, and so I went alone. I felt dwarfed and alone in the big church as I listened to Max's son-in-law tell how magnificently Max had presided at his granddaughter's wedding only a few weeks earlier. After the ceremony, Max had called out a Hawaiian chant to "Pele." At the time, the nontraditional chanting by his unusual father-in-law pastor had seemed embarrassing. Now his son-in-law was grateful for it. He also spoke of Minnie and gave her the highest compliment. "Childless Minnie," he said, "became a mother to us all."

After the funeral, I went to the little cemetery near the small Methodist church where Max and Minnie were buried side by side. A short distance away, I saw the burial place of Ruth, Max's first wife, and I remembered how Minnie and Max almost broke off their engagement over their disagreement concerning where Max would be buried. Max had always expected to be buried next to Ruth. However, Minnie said, that if that were the case, she would not marry Max.

Finally, Max relented, "Where I will be buried is *not* going to be the reason for whether we marry."

Good theology, Max. He understood that it was not a matter of loyalty to Ruth's memory. Minnie just wanted to make sure that Max was fully committed to her. Since they died together, it was fitting they were buried together.

* * * * *

I drove home from the double funeral in an unrelenting heavy rainstorm making my way through soaking, vicious Chicago traffic. As I drove, frequently stepping on the brakes, barely able to see through the rain-splattered windshield, I couldn't help think about Minnie. Max had planned his funeral carefully, with hymn selections and scriptures to be read. He had meticulously laid out his funeral service knowing Minnie and his family would follow it, but never considered the possibility of a double funeral. It was a perfect funeral for Max, but what about Minnie?

Oh, no! "The Red River Valley!" I had forgotten!

In my shock and grief, I had completely forgotten that Minnie had wanted "Red River Valley" sung at her funeral. She had told me so at the cabin only a few months before she died. At that time, I thought she was kidding, but she was serious. How could I not have remembered? I had let Minnie down. I had let my friend down!

Driving through endless rain-streaked hopeless knots of cars, looking for loopholes and wanting a strawberry ice cream cone more than anything in the world, I began singing through my tears:

From this Valley they say you are going.
I will miss your bright eyes and sweet
smile.
For they say you are taking the sunshine
That brightened my pathway awhile.

* * * * *

Before her life ended, Minnie may have had at least a subconscious awareness that she might die soon. Our "Red River Valley" talk was one of those conversations that suggest more is happening than words alone convey. In retrospect, although he may not have wanted to leave this earth quite so soon, Max seemed ready to "go," "pass on," die. He had a strong Christian faith and was prepared for his earthly Max-life to end. His life was complete; he had met his goals.

On the other hand, *if* to live or die was a subconscious choice for Minnie—to be escorted by Max into the next life, or continue living in a disabled body, Minnie would choose to go with Max. Four dips!

Sometimes we see clues, times when, for a nanosecond, the present, past, and future come together. Minnie's fall off the bike seemed like such a moment—when a flash of realization that her physical abilities had dwindled, and her body potentially could become severely compromised.

Max, Romeo; Minnie, Juliet; two seniors from different backgrounds who came together, who lived together and died together, "really/truly" a love story, but that's not the ending. Their spiritual existence continues.

Minnie and Max Kemling, 1987

24

Asta ('Ah-stah)

"Welcome, Kmart shoppers," intoned a shopping-god voice over the loudspeaker, and I felt mercifully welcome.

It was Easter Sunday afternoon. My mother was dying, and this was the second time in the last four weeks my husband and I had flown from Chicago to Birmingham, this trip accompanied by my younger son Noah. Hospice nurses had said more than once that my mother had only a short time to live, but they were not correct. "Not more than a week," one would say or "probably only another night." But Mother would rally, and as soon as she would rally, the nurses would have to leave due to hospice protocol. Meanwhile, the horrific pain of her bone cancer was becoming unbearable for her. No medication seemed to control the pain; doses of morphine made her crazy. Like several other members of our family, Mother was not going "gentle into that good night."

I pushed my mother's wheelchair through a few Kmart aisles. "Want to look at some robes?" I questioned. She nodded.

I held up a blue flowered robe, then a simpler white one. She held one, and then the other, fingering the fabric. My mother had been an excellent seamstress and for years sewed most of my clothes. I still wear a skirt she made for me.

"This one is pretty," I said, as if I were a salesperson. Mother looked at me like I had lost my mind.

"Not good." She was right. The fabric was of inferior quality, but if I were dying, would I consider whether it might shrink?

It had been only two months since my mother had left the retirement home in Grand Island, Nebraska, to come and stay temporarily with my sister Karma and her teenage daughter, my niece, Thais. The facility where my mother lived was not licensed for hospice patients, and although she was terminally ill, Mom was neither sufficiently ill nor willing to go into the nursing wing. But here, in a strange city, she had declined rapidly.

"I want to go," she had kept saying as the cancer advanced throughout her body. "I want to go. Let's go!"

"Where do you want to go?"

She would respond with a puzzled look; she had no idea.

This Easter morning, she had said it again, "I want to go. Let's go!"

"Where do you want to go?"

To our surprise, she answered, "Shopping."

Shopping? That was impossible. Mom was bedridden most of the time, and on heavy drugs. But my sister Karma, who was then chairperson of the theater department at the University of Alabama, has a way of doing the impractical, sometimes the impossible. "Let's do it. Let's take her shopping!" she said.

My mother smiled through the drugs.

"You're kidding," I said. "She's too ill. What if something happens?"

"What if it does?" Karma asked.

"Anyway, where will we go? It's Easter Sunday."

"Kmart. I'll bet Kmart is open."

"We'll have to carry her in the wheelchair all the way down the steps." My sister's apartment was a second-story apartment requiring negotiation of outside cement stairs.

"We can do it!" my son Noah said.

Kmart was calling us. Everyone was ready to go; it was much better than sitting around. The whole business of life-ending had become tedious, boring, depressing.

"Let's go shopping!"

Three men—Don, Noah, and Karma's husband, Dan—were able to carry my mother in a wheelchair down the stairs. Mother cried out only once, biting down on her lip, as they moved her into the front seat of the car. Off we went—a few blocks, and now we were at Kmart.

My sister and niece helped find a nicer robe of quality fabric—to Mother's satisfaction.

"Anything else?" I asked. "Shall we head for the cashier?"

Mother nodded.

One of mother's habits that I found embarrassing was the way she would engage cashiers in personal and lengthy conversations. In our other visits, she might have told the cashier, "My daughter and her husband are visiting from Chicago," or "This is my daughter who works for the university. She doesn't live far from here." I thought most cashiers didn't care whether or not we were visiting, or if my sister taught at the university. But Mother saw every clerk as a new friend with whom to share something about her life. Now it was I who wanted to say to the clerk, "*My mother here is dying, and she wanted to come here, to this Kmart, the very last time she will probably ever get outside in this world to buy anything. Actually, she was supposed to have died two weeks ago, but she wasn't ready.*"

Of course, I could not have said it. We all were barely holding it together.

"Do you want to go home or take a drive in the country?" Karma asked Mom.

"Let's go…" Mother said, but then to our surprise, she added, "home."

✶ ✶ ✶ ✶ ✶

Two weeks later, Don and I, along with my son Mitch, flew once again back to Birmingham. Mother was in bed and very weak, completely quiet. Again the nurses had left because Mom had stabilized. She seemed to know us, but she was in so much pain, so uncomfortable in spite of the morphine inside her body that it was nearly impossible to communicate.

My sister said, "I think part of her has already gone. One night, when I was sitting here, someone or something came for her, and part of her left. I think I saw someone come to fetch her and part of her leave."

Perhaps, I thought. *We know so little.*

"Why don't you get out of here for a while?" I said to Karma. She and her daughter, Thais, had been caring for Mother night and day for several weeks. "I'll stay with Mom." I said. "You take a walk."

Karma at first protested, and then realized she needed to get away and left to take a long walk.

As I sat there reading a book, Mother finally slept. She was truly resting. All afternoon, I sat with her, reading a little, watching over her, grateful she was able to rest. Occasionally, her grandchildren and my husband, Don, would come into the room. "Oh, good! She's finally sleeping!" they would say, glad she was no longer trying to go, to escape—whether from death or toward it, we did not know.

Late in the afternoon, the hospice nurse telephoned. "How is your mother?"

"She's resting very well," I said. "She's very quiet. She's sleeping!"

"Are you sure? Could she be in a coma?"

I was startled. "I don't know. How do you tell? She *is* in a deep sleep."

"I'll be right over."

The nurse was right. Mother was in a light coma.

The final vigil began. We moved in and out of her room, holding her hand, speaking to her, but with little response. Still she stayed. She did not go. Why didn't she go?

At eleven that night, my son Mitch came in the room to tell me that my daughter Thea had telephoned from Chicago. "Thea called. She says Bedstemor [Grandmother] needs a service."

It was late at night. In Birmingham, my mother, who had served in the church as the minister's wife all her adult life, was without a clergyman.

"We don't know anyone here." I said. "What does Thea mean she needs a service?" It was a request I would not have expected from my daughter.

"I don't know. That's what she says."

Slowly, another hour went by. My daughter called again from Chicago. Now, it was midnight. Again she told my son to tell me. "Bedstemor needs a service."

"Okay," I said. "All right. Okay. We'll do it." Why was I reluctant to assume a clergy role for my mother when I would not have hesitated for someone else? "Where's Dad's old ministerial book?"

From a bottom drawer, my sister took out the thin black book with my father's penciled European handwriting in the margin and handed it to me. I opened it.

"We're going to have a service for Bedstemor," I said.

We gathered around her bed—Mitch, Karma, Thais, Don, myself. I believe others we could not see were also present.

First, I read from Psalm 32, which seemed appropriate given her bone cancer:

> Happy are those whose transgressions are forgiven, And whose sin is put away!
> Happy are they to whom the Lord imputes no guilt, and in whose spirit there is no guile!
> While I held my tongue, my bones withered away, Because of my groaning all day long.
> For your hand was heavy upon me day and night; My moisture was dried up as in the heat of summer. Then I acknowledged my sin to you, And did not conceal my guilt.
> I said, "I will confess my transgression to the Lord" Then he forgave me the guilt of my sin.
> Be glad, you righteous, and rejoice in the Lord; Shout for joy, you who are true of heart.

My mother was righteous and true of heart! We could shout for joy for her! I made the sign of the cross on her forehead: "In the name of the Father

311

and of the Son and of the Holy Spirit. I forgive you all your sins. The Lord bless you and keep you. The Lord make His face shine upon you and be gracious unto you. The Lord lift up his countenance upon you and give you peace. Amen."

We stood in a circle around my mother's bed, holding each other's hands, including Mother's. She sat forward, holding on to us. Although she was in a coma, she was very much present. Mother, Bedstemor, was with us.

Each of us spoke to her:

"Mom, I love you so much…You have been a wonderful mother."

"I will miss you, and I will miss your music so much. But I know you will have the angels singing as they have never sung before! Heaven will be blessed by your music. It will never be the same again."

"Thank you…Thank you for all you have done for us."

"I love you, Bedstemor…Go in peace. All of us here love you, and we are so grateful to you."

"We will miss you, Bedstemor. I love you, Bedstemor."

"You can go now," Thais said.

And we laughed.

We decided to sing a Danish song for her, and we chose one she had played a million times, one we sang as children and as young adults, a song which had been translated for us by her uncle, "Evening Star":

Evening star up yonder,
Teach me like you to wander
Willing and obediently
The path that God ordained for me
Evening star up yonder.[1]

We ended with the Lord's Prayer, and when we
finished, Mother lay back down on her pillows and
was very quiet. We all left the room except for my
sister, who lay down on the floor by Mother's bed.
Don and I lay down on the living room floor in our
sleeping bags. It was one in the morning. An hour
later my sister woke me.

"She's gone," my sister said.

"Gone?"

"Yes," she said. "Just a few minutes ago."

Gone. Asta Juhl Ibsen had finally been able to
go. Thea had been right. Somehow, my mother from
her coma, or someone on her behalf, had transmit-
ted the message to her granddaughter in Chicago.
Mother needed a service to be able to go. Now she
was gone. Exactly the right word. Not dead. Gone.

We went in to say goodbye. Each of us took the
time we needed. A while later, two men came in an
ambulance for her body.

"You may want to go out on the balcony," the
nurse said. "It may be upsetting to see her body leave."

Out on the balcony in the cool Alabama spring
air, I stood with members of my family and looked
down at the night world. People. Trees. Cars. Noise.
Grass. Flowers. A siren. Earth things. As we stood

there silently together, the men placed her body in a black bag and carried it out to the ambulance. None of us cried. Our mother wasn't in that black bag. She had left already.

The rest of the night we sat up and talked. My sister and I sorted through some of her jewelry, "I'll make a special box of jewelry for us and one for each of her granddaughters," my sister said. I nodded.

It was only seven o'clock when we left for the airport—Don, Mitch, and I boarded a flight back to Chicago. Half sick from too much coffee and too little sleep, I stared out the window of the plane, looking into the early morning clouds. Where did my mother go? Was she out there somewhere, flying around in the clouds? It was a silly thought, but now that my mother had gone, was completely out of reach, I wondered where she was. I wanted to reach out of the airplane window and touch her once more. But she had completely vanished.

On the funeral bulletin, we had printed the last verse of "Evening Star":

> Evening Sun descending
> Teach me when life is ending
> Night shall pass and I, like you,
> Shall rise again, where life is new!
> Teach me, sun descending![1]

* * * * *

Mom died in 1993—a long time ago. In the months that followed, I experienced a much deeper grief than expected, a grief that would catch me unaware. It was like falling through a trap door, stepping on an emotional land mine that would go off unexpectedly. I might be at a dinner with friends, driving home from work, or at a concert when I would suddenly fall into an emotional pit, uncontrollable tears, engulfed by bottomless grief. If I was with others, I would excuse myself and find a place of privacy. What was happening to me? What could possibly explain such deep sorrow over my mother's life-ending? Asta Juhl Ibsen was eighty-five years old when she died. She didn't like being ill or old; she was ready to die. Patience was not her strong suit, and once terminally ill, she was as impatient about dying as she was in life. Although I felt closer to my father than my mother, I felt bereft and was considerably more emotional when my mom died.

The ending of my mother's life meant the loss of her high-spirited music. Could I breathe without it? Mother's inimitable style of playing the piano and organ expressed her way of approaching life—creative, courageous, supportive, appreciative, passionate, good natured, exultant. I know of no other musician that made that same sound, a mixture of Lutheran hymns, Danish folk songs, and New Orleans jazz.

Mother's funeral was at St. John's Lutheran Church in Kronborg, Nebraska, the last church my dad and she had served, taught school, and where she had continued to live with many friends. I wanted Mother's music to be part of her funeral, and so I had a technician in Chicago splice selections of her playing the piano and organ to be played over a loud-speaker as people entered the church for the funeral service. When people came into the funeral home, they stopped to listen. "Why, that's…that's Asta playing!"

The wife of the undertaker came into the funeral parlor, asking, "Where did that music come from? It's beautiful!"

A stranger, whose child had been in one of my mother's classrooms, shook my hand with Nebraska heartiness, "If a child had even a tiny bit of music in 'em, your mother would reach way down inside 'em, grab it and she'd git it out!"

The word *Asta* means "star"; she was a guiding star for us. I am unsure why I felt such deep grief following my mother's death. I did not want her to be in pain, and I knew her spirit would continue. Mother considered dying a necessary obligation, and she went about it bravely with little emotion. We were equally obligated to let her go. But after she was gone, I felt incredibly alone. No one loves you the same way as your mother. It is a terrible loss.

Grief can become an endless waterwheel. If there is no bottom to grief, a person sometimes has to construct one, a platform in order not to keep churn-ing around in it. That was what I had to do.

As my sister and I stepped to the head of the family's matriarchal line, I needed to make changes.

I had to build an escape kit. My heart's desire was "to write and do some music." It wasn't going to happen as long as I had a job that consumed me in Chicago, even though there was much I enjoyed about my work. I decided to retire at the age of sixty. Meanwhile, I would begin preparing a home in the Upper Peninsula of Michigan, where several friends had moved.

My mother left each of her children $23,000, and with my inheritance I bought a hundred-year-old home in a small town (an entire large house on three lots). Naturally, it needed a great deal of work, but it had promise.

I was not alone in my pursuit to go to the north woods. A few blocks away from the hospital where I worked a good friend, Charlotte, also wanted to move to the Upper Peninsula of Michigan. It was a dream we shared, and one I had every expectation would become a reality for both of us. For Charlotte, it was going to be too late.

Mother visited us at Rocky Shores, our cabin on Lake Superior, in the fall a few years before she died. Immediately she walked out to the lake, using her cane. To this day, I try to see the beauty of the fall leaves through her eyes. "Isn't that *beautiful?*" she would say with such excitement that I would take another look at the tree in order to really see it. Yes, it really is *beautiful!*

Asta Juhl Ibsen

25

Charlotte

I retired at the end of the year 2000. Don and I had been preparing our home in the Upper Peninsula for five years—torn down the icehouse, a second chimney, built a new garage, brought heat and plumbing into the upstairs, added a new large bathroom, insulation, new siding, and a deck. There was still a lot of work to be done, including remodeling the kitchen, but the house was ready to be occupied.

In June, we moved our furniture to Michigan. I returned to work at Swedish Covenant Hospital. At the end of the month, as a member of the Management Council, I voted yes (it was a unanimous approval) for the hospital to proceed with heart surgery. On July 5th, Don had a test at the hospital, which to our shock, revealed that he needed a triple bypass operation, the first such operation at Swedish Covenant Hospital. To complicate matters, I was renting a room for the remainder of the year from my friend, Corinne Murphy Hines who was administratively responsible for the cardiology department, and Don also would be living in her home for a month following surgery until he could travel.

After he moved from intensive care, Don's first visitor in the hospital was our friend Charlotte, who lived only a few blocks from the hospital. Charlotte hated hospitals and made no attempt to disguise her distrust. She harbored an impenetrable grudge against the corporate world, including hospitals. But as soon as visitors were allowed, Charlotte was at Don's bedside with her support and helpful suggestions.

* * * * *

Charlotte's plan to move to the UP included her purchase of a small cottage in Kenton, a town five miles away from our home in Trout Creek. The next fall while visiting us, she told me, rather shyly, that she had been to a gynecologist for the first time in many years, and the doctor had told her bluntly she had cancer. The doctor went on, cruelly, to say it was her own fault for waiting too long to seek medical help. There was nothing that could be done. She was going to die.

Charlotte was very angry. Not for one minute did she accept such a callous pronouncement. Shaken, at first she cried alone, then told her husband, John, and finally her two older children, Nicky and Anna, who wept along with her. She did not tell her youngest son, Hiam, a developmentally delayed teenager who had recently graduated from high school. Instead she set about her task of proving the doctor wrong by finding a physician who gave her hope and treated her like a real person. As for Hiam, he knew something definitely was wrong.

"Mom's real sick," he said to me over the telephone.

At our wedding, Charlotte had presented Don and me with two large bags of her famous health food meals, which I feared I would dislike. The collection of mysterious jars of greenish food did not have an especially pleasant look. But when I opened each jar and tried morsel after morsel, I found it was delicious!

Charlotte's interest in health, her concern for avoiding illness and improving body movement was unrelenting. "Promise me you won't go down that stairway with the dog!" she had said the last time she visited us in Michigan. I was startled. What was this about?

"You can fall! That's how people get hurt. Always make sure the dog is at the bottom of the stairway *before* you go down."

"Okay. Okay," I said although I saw no danger whatsoever in the possibility of my falling over the dog and down the stairs.

While I rarely have head colds, when I did come down with one, it was a doozy. Charlotte was tenacious. "Are you drinking enough liquids? What are you eating?"

"How do you feel?" she would ask after a Feldenkrais treatment in her studio, where I learned to became increasingly aware of discreet muscle groups I never knew existed.

"Better," I said. "Much better," and I would look into the long mirrors covering one studio wall: I *was* straighter, taller, my face looked refreshed, relaxed, younger.

"You look great!" she said, satisfied. "Now, walk!" (I have a somewhat awkward gait.) "See, you're walking better too!"

A few months after her initial disclosure, Charlotte visited us once more in Michigan. When I asked how it was going, she said, "I don't want to talk about it. I don't want advice!"

A person working on a miracle can't afford advice.

For a while, Charlotte seemed fine in our telephone conversations and e-mails, but she canceled her next two visits. When she canceled the second one, I knew Charlotte was really sick.

* * * * *

Another summer came, and Don and I decided to take a vacation to Colorado, where he had grown up. He missed the Rocky Mountains; I loved them too.

After a day of exploring the Garden of the Gods in Colorado Springs, I picked up the neatly printed note in the lobby of the once old hotel in Manitou

Springs, now a bed-and-breakfast. The note read, "*Call Charlotte.*"

Receiving a message like that on vacation is never good news. My friend Charlotte was in need. "How are you doing?" I asked stupidly when she answered the telephone.

"What do you mean, how am I doing? I'm in shock! That's not why I am calling…Can you… can you help us?" I understood then what she wanted. She was asking for help in paying the bills. Charlotte and her husband were alternative health practitioners, uninsured, and unprepared for a catastrophic health situation. John, her legally blind husband, managed a limited practice in massage work and kinesiology. They both helped people maintain and recover their health, while distant from the mainstream medical system.

"I'll do what I can," I promised, knowing there was little I could do. Established policies at hospitals dictate financial matters. Nevertheless, I called administrator friends at the hospital to do as much as possible, and then turned to my husband. "I want to see Charlotte. I need to see her. Let's go home through Chicago."

Don and I took a long detour, driving home through Chicago. We found Charlotte at home propped up on a temporary bed in her dining room, weak, thin, and determined more than ever. After an exchange of greetings and catching up on our families, I tried to address the problem of her obtaining the care she needed. "You need to be thinking about hospice care," I said, a betrayal to my friend's need to believe that the cancer was retreating and would never claim victory over her. We both believed in miracles. How could I be letting her down?

Charlotte looked up at me, her penetrating Italian brown eyes staring through me as if to say, *Et tu brute?* "Do *you* think I'm going to die?" she asked sharply. It was a reprimand.

I hesitated, realizing I had a choice. I could say, "Of course you aren't going to die. You are too young, and your husband and children need you too much. God is not that unfair. You eat only healthy food. You are the best cook of natural food that ever lived. You don't smoke or drink and you stay away from dangerous chemicals. You voted for Ralph Nader. You never let your children eat anything but fresh food, broccoli and wild rice, organic milk and beef. We need you, Charlotte. You can't die!"

Or I could have been loyal to our code of honesty and say, "Charlotte, your cancer has advanced. You are in terrible pain. You can't even hold up your head or turn your body without help! You can't feed yourself, and you are so weak your son has to carry you down the basement stairs to the shower. You are wearing diapers! Face it, Charlotte! It is getting too hard to take care of you. John is exhausted and unable to work. You have to confront this!"

But I could not say that either.

Did I think she was dying? Yes, but Charlotte could not give up. Her inability to give up had brought her many victories. Hiam had been extremely ill as an infant with little muscle tone in his frail body. In spite of what doctors said, she had insisted he would have a normal life. Her refusal to accept anything less was a major reason Hiam finally learned to crawl, then walk and talk, attend high school, play the piano, the saxophone, make movies and play drums. If you wanted to be a friend of Charlotte's, you must be Hiam's friend first. How could she possibly leave Hiam now, just as he was entering the adult world and needing her as much as ever?

"You don't have to die in order to have hospice care," I reasoned. "But you *are* very ill and need a lot of help. You could fool them!" I added brightly.

Charlotte didn't smile. She knew I had betrayed her. "My Chinese doctor says he has brought back people who are sicker than I am," she said, now angry and disappointed by my lack of confidence.

"That's good," I said. Had her doctor really brought people who were more ill than Charlotte back to health? I believed in miracles, but they don't always happen just because we demand them. Often they are unexpected. When to believe in miracles and when to face "reality"?

"I'd like some more tea," Charlotte said. Likely, the blends of teas and herbs prescribed by alternative Chinese medicine were helping her as much as Western medicine could, and with fewer side effects. I went to the kitchen for tea. When I came back, I held it to her lips, holding her up with my free arm so she could drink.

"Good," I said as she took a few sips, "that's good."

When we left, I knew I would never see her alive again.

The trip back home was glum. How would I ever do without her friendship? A small part of me believed that somehow there would be a miracle. Apparently, Charlotte also occasionally wavered. A mutual friend told me that in the hospital, John encouraged her to eat her broccoli because it would help her.

"Fuck the broccoli," Charlotte said.

* * * * *

A few weeks after our return to Michigan, I received a call that Charlotte was again hospitalized. The doctors did not expect her to make it through the weekend. The miracle was not going to happen.

I called the familiar telephone number of the hospital where I had worked for so many years, the hospital close to Charlotte's home where we had often met for walks and talks, usually outside at noon on the hospital steps, since Charlotte didn't want to set foot inside. Now she was confined in a place she hated but desperately needed, helpless in a hospital bed about to die. The telephone rang in her room, and to my surprise, I was able to speak with her.

"Hello," I said. "Are they taking good care of you?"

"Yes. Yes they are."

"They better…I've been calling people."

"I know."

"I am sending you all the love and blessings in the world," I said.

"Thank you."

"Love you…"

"Goodbye," Charlotte said very slowly. I knew it was really the end. She had not said, "See you," or "Take care." She had said, "Goodbye."

A few days before her life ended, Hiam was finally told how ill his mother was. He accepted it matter-of-factly; perhaps he had known all along.

Don and I came back to Chicago for the funeral in the Anthroposophic Church. Instead of a funeral home, her body was in a room in the church basement. Friends and clients brought voluminous plates and baskets of delicious healthy food. No cake-mix cakes. No bakery-bought sugar cookies. Tables in the church basement were covered with platters of fresh fruit, brown rice, organic vegetables, homemade breads, and heaping salads full of pine nuts.

Charlotte's friends and family penned original poems and remembrances in a special book of heartfelt tributes. Many adults as well as children drew pictures. Rows of photographs of Charlotte's life decorated one wall—Charlotte as an infant with brother and parents; Charlotte in her wedding dress; Charlotte with her babies, her greatest triumph. How she reveled in motherhood!

Nicky, her political-activist carpenter son, had constructed a splendid coffin—fashioned from beautiful pine, lovingly stained and polished, with smooth corners and exquisite carvings, lined with old lace.

Somehow, he had miraculously constructed it during one very long day. In a darkened room, adjoining the fellowship hall, candles burned brightly and red roses reposed in the loving coffin cradling Charlotte's body.

A handmade coffin. What a sendoff! Charlotte, like a baby chick, lay patiently in a hand-carved wooden egg—about to hatch, about to continue her healing work, newborn, in another place, in another way. I knew it. Charlotte was and is a healer.

I think of her constantly when I am on the stairs. One thing Charlotte can be sure of. I'll never fall over the dog.

$$* * * * *$$

Years after Charlotte's life ended, I am still surprised whenever a health-conscious friend succumbs to a sudden illness such as cancer or a heart attack. We are responsible for our own health, but we are definitely not totally in control.

Why *did* Charlotte die so young? Perhaps if she did not have the distain for doctors and the medical model, her cancer could have been caught earlier and given her several more years. We need to live holistically, balance alternative with medical health. Or perhaps Charlotte needed to "let go," and dying was the only way that could be accomplished. It could also be that she was needed wherever souls go—to continue her coaching, her healing work, in another dimension. That also was a goal of Charlotte's.

I won't be surprised to see her again and to take some more lessons from her.

Charlotte Palumbo belly dancing

26

John Mitchell

In 1939, a little boy in Baltimore was about to cross the street on his way to school when he suddenly turned and ran back home to his aging Aunt Maggie. "Mitch!" she said, "What are you doing back home?"

"I forgot my report card," Mitch said, grabbing a gold-colored envelope off the table in the entrance of their row house. Already a day late, his report card boasted mostly "O's" for "Outstanding" with just one or two "S's" for "Satisfactory." His educator parents were so proud of Mitch; their other two sons, one burdened by severe dyslexia and the other by a genius IQ, did not do as well as Mitch in school.

The little boy darted out of the house, lunch pail in one hand, report card in the other. If he ran as fast as he could, he would not be tardy; that too appeared in report cards. No time to go all the way to the corner of the block. Running like a gigantic insect, his long arms and legs flagellating from where they connected to his torso, Mitch ran midblock across the street—right into the path of a delivery truck. He never saw it.

His full name was John Mitchell Martin, and in the family tradition, he was called by his middle name, Mitch, for his mother's family, who were said to be descendants of the Mitchells from Virginia. His father was called Lee; his name was Arthur Lee, the last of three sons who together bore the name: Robert, Edward, Lee, revealing ancestral Southern sympathies.

Because John Mitchell's small angular skull was fractured, a steel plate was inserted at the top of his head, and for weeks he lay in a coma; his elderly great aunt, Maggie Grimm, sat at his bedside and held his hand by the hour, waiting, praying that he would come out of the coma. If only she had reminded him to look both ways as he ran out of the house. Living in her nephew's household was the right of an elderly maiden aunt; she was obligated to the family for care and protection of the children. She had failed in her duties.

Arthur Lee had a sterner view. "Mitch should have looked both ways! It was his fault. He should know better!" As John Mitchell's father and principal of a junior high school, Lee should have taught his son to be tougher. Mitch was far too sensitive for a boy. Many children brought their report cards back late. It was no reason to put your life in jeopardy. He must toughen the boy up.

Mildred, Mitch's mother, came to the hospital every day after teaching school, relieving Maggie, who sat with Mitch during the day. Lee's indictment of their son bothered her; she argued in her son's behalf. "Mitch was in a hurry. The driver was going too fast!" But Mildred also felt guilty for Mitch's near fatal accident. Mitch was the favorite of her three sons; she found his sweet personality irresistible. Perhaps God was punishing her for favoring one of her children.

To the doctors' surprise, after three months, Mitch came out of the coma. He simply woke up and came back to earth, although his beautiful brain had sustained multiple injuries. At nearly seven years of age, he had the task of learning to walk all over again.

Aunt Maggie thanked God and resolved to be more attentive to the children's care. "Wear a hat. Don't be in such a hurry. Drink your orange juice. Do you have your papers for school? Be careful when you cross the street."

Mildred decided she had been mistaken— God wasn't punishing her after all. Her middle son would always have a special place in her heart. Now he needed her attention and love more than ever so he could learn to walk again, catch up with his schoolwork, gain confidence. Lee, too, had been given another chance. He now had an opportunity to toughen Mitch up—through physical and verbal beatings. "What's the matter with you?" he would say and get out his belt. "I'll teach you…" But Mitch did not become tougher; he simply developed a shell of charm, good humor, and charisma—one in which he could crawl into and hide, sufficiently large to accommodate his elongated body and a self-image that relied on constant polishing. He grew to be handsome, long-armed, and six feet six inches tall. The steel plate in his head did not show.

In the next fifty years, the lives of first Mildred, then Maggie, and finally Arthur Lee all ended. Eventually, it was John Mitchell's turn. Mitch, the boy with so much promise, bright, sweet, good-looking Mitch, who had unexpectedly survived a pedestrian accident, the first graduate of Catonsville Community College, president of Shimer College's honor's society and the Green Curtain Theatre club, charismatic actor and talented poet. Life should have gone very well for him, but it did not. He, beating the odds, meticulously sabotaged his careers as teacher, newspaperman, writer, and actor, running away from each impending success like it was a report card needing to be returned, dashing headlong into more comfortable failure, manufacturing rationales of "principles" whenever an advancement came close. Perhaps it was to taunt his principal father, perhaps for another reason or maybe no reason at all. Increasingly he swabbed his ego with alcohol. One way or another, he would become spectacular—either a tremendous success or a colossal failure; John Mitchell abhorred mediocrity.

He was a terrible husband to two wives, each of whom loved and believed in him; he abandoned his three children financially and emotionally "for their own good," ignoring their birthdays, holidays, graduations, and basic attention. He bolted from a master's degree one course before completion and resigned in anger from more than one job to prevent a pending promotion. After years of flinging himself between alcoholism and mental health problems, he found refuge in Alcoholics Anonymous and then Gamblers Anonymous. His response to AA treatment was a brand of orthodox insanity. He lived only twenty-four hours at a time and would make no commitments for anything exceeding that length of time. Apologizing was something John Mitchell came to consider unprincipled excuses, and he avoided all expressions of gratitude for the many kindnesses bestowed him. He chose extreme poverty, claiming material success was a sign of ultimate weakness.

But through all this, John, for the most part, preserved his laser-sharp precepts and insights, his artistic ability to craft winsome poems, a high regard for logic and precise language, a belly-laughing sense of humor, an occasional splash of sacrificial kindness, and an outlandish criticism of social hypocrisy. John Mitchell was an uncompromising spirit and fun to be around. Many people loved him.

John died as he had lived his last thirty years, poor, with as few material goods as possible. Pancreatic cancer necessitated placement in a nursing home that accepted hardship cases. He called for help from a few homeless friends camping out in his subsidized apartment, asking them to help him escape. He wasn't going to stay in the nursing home and add to their conspiracy of accepting state aid for his less than adequate care. John and his helpers were successful; they managed to free him, but in less than twenty-four hours, terminally ill, he was forced to return, but to a different nursing home.

This time there was no escape. John's children, Thea, Mitch, and Noah, traveled long distances to see him, to bring flowers and clean underwear, to search for those traces of the father they had known as children before life with him became madness— his warmth, his fun, his sardonic wisdom, his laugh, his uncompromising ways. They couldn't help but still care for him. Forgiveness was not the issue of the moment. John Mitchell did not express regret for not supporting them or giving even minimal attention. Should they be thankful or angry their father had abandoned them? John was convinced they should be thankful. If they weren't, that was their problem.

* * * * *

John Mitchell Martin died Memorial Day weekend in 2002. A few days later, his family and friends met in his favorite coffee shop in Rock Island, Illinois, preparing to distribute his ashes in the Mississippi River before the memorial service. Longtime friend and director of the local antipoverty community organization, Vince Thomas, an incomprehensibly kind man from India, led the funeral troop procession. Now, simply called by his first name, John had quit his part-time public relations job numerous times, only for Vince to rehire him each time. Vince had arranged for John's housing and health care, notified his family when John became ill, and finally made funeral arrangements.

On the first but not last uncomfortable day of summer they walked, across the hot muggy streets of downtown Rock Island. John's children carried his ashes. Vince led, followed by Thea, John's daughter; Mitch, his older son and namesake, with daughter-in-law, Susan; Noah, his younger son, accompanied by his fiancé, Christine; John's ex-wife (me), with my husband, Don; two of John's former girlfriends; a camera man, a newspaper colleague, a friend of John's daughter; a writer pal from former days; a young musician wearing a suit, a delicate-looking young girl pushing her baby in a stroller; and finally a few anonymous AA and former gambler friends. They walked past new and old stores keeping a semblance of their line together as they maneuvered around shoppers, down to the Mississippi River, past the casino where John Mitchell had lost whatever money he "came by."

The entourage followed the pied piper from India, single file, north on the causeway along the steep Mississippi riverbank. Vince had come early that morning to pick up the beer cans thrown the previous evening. Almost every member of the parade carried a rose: Thea had purchased large beautiful roses for the funeral procession to throw into the river. I asked for the singular yellow rose among the red, luscious pink and glowing peach roses my daughter offered each of us. During our marriage, John would never remember Valentine's Day (he considered it a Hallmark conspiracy) or give me the gift of red roses. But for many years, he wrote a special poem for me and presented it on February 15, which was The Feast of Lupercalia, the ancient Roman festival held to promote fertility and ward off disasters. And once, he gave me a bouquet of yellow roses.

At the side of the Moline riverbank, older son, Lee Mitchell read a poem John had written about standing in the sun and having a shadow—proof of his existence.

"Let's sing 'Amazing Grace,'" Mitch suggested, since the poem was so short and to the point. In the hot baking June sun, the group sang the first verse as best they could, then individually we climbed down steep broken steps to the old Mississippi.

John's son Mitch, then his daughter Thea, and finally his younger son Noah, each tossed in a rose and emptied some of John's ashes from a plastic bag into the Mississippi River. The fine ash powdered into the wind before temporarily muddying a small part of the ancient river.

Then the others, one by one each, balanced on a rock and tossed a rose into the water, then stood silently for a moment watching the rose make its way downstream. Some said a little goodbye prayer or recalled how they would always remember John.

It was my turn, I who had once "plighted my troth" to John. I tossed in the yellow rose. Thoughts were too complicated, memories too vast, emotions too jumbled to give form. I simply watched the rose depart. It was all so ordinary—before the extraordinary occurred.

We watched as the yellow rose reversed its direction—turning, returning, coming resolutely back toward the shore against the current, across Mississippi River wavelets, counter-crossing, and maneuvering over an abyss of water.

I heard someone say, "Look! It's coming back!"

A mixture of emotions collided within me—fascination, fear, astonishment, surprise, familiarity, recognition—so perfectly apt, so much like him. Had he (it) forgotten something? Floating, floating ever nearer the shore, the yellow rose seemed to be returning with a final message, returning to say…what…what was he (it) saying? Does such a message have sound? Can such communication be articulated?

Alarmed, my husband, Don, also saw what was happening. He picked up a nearby branch and tried to redirect the yellow rose so it would float downstream, as was natural, meant to be. But the rose was approaching the shore! Standing beside me, Don tried again to send it downstream by poking it with his branch. But the yellow rose persisted until it lodged itself in the rocks near the shore. Now, risking a fall into the river, almost desperately Don reached the rose with the branch, pushed it, and nearly toppled into the water.

Could this be on camera? It might win a prize on the home video network if Don fell into the river.

Against all reason, the yellow rose had returned, but dislodged by the branch, it obediently left—silently flowing downstream like the enchanting Ophelia.

Can the song of the yellow rose be heard? What is its melody? If there were words that I heard, they might have been, "Aloha...hello...Goodbye...I love you...I'm sorry...I'm not sorry...Aloha."

* * * * *

Following the ceremony of the ashes and the river, a reception for John was held in the Project Now offices, the same agency I had attempted to help during Model Cities "Citizen Participation" days. In the thirty years that had passed, the agency had grown tremendously and was now large and successful, administering a number of programs and grants. John's friends, coworkers, and family gathered for potluck.

Friends spoke candidly about John, beginning with the many times during the past few years when he had quit his part-time job and again been rehired at Project Now. A CD of John reading his poetry played, reminding me of our theatrical days. Many people gave tributes, including a former student of his from the time we taught at St. Katherine's/St. Mark's, which, in hindsight, had been one of the best times of our marriage. A number of lonely and handicapped people in the audience spoke about the help John had given them, how he would stay with them when they needed someone. The young man in a suit said, "He was like a father to me," causing John's bio-logical son Noah to look greatly puzzled. A friend of John's who did not know I was in attendance said, "John Martin would never tolerate anything negative being said about his ex-wife."

John's lack of living up to society's demands as a provider, a teacher, a good parent, and an attentive husband seemed almost inconsequential that after-noon. He met the needs of several people who knew him as a fellow traveler; they didn't try to make him any different from who he was. There was no need.

When I met John, I was a twenty-year-old ide-alist, my life was before me. John Mitchell Martin was older, a married man, and at the time, I had no interest in getting involved with him or anyone else. When I married him three years later, I had no idea of the difficult future that lay before us; it became much worse than my mind could conceive as pos-sible, even when I tried to think of "the worst that could happen." If I had been more aware, I could have avoided the pain of our marriage, but then I would not have the profound joy our three children have brought me, and I may have lived my entire life in a complacent, superficial understanding of life and love; John made that impossible.

John Mitchell Martin, Faculty,
St. Katharine's/St. Mark's

JOY IBSEN

The Last Feast of Lupercalia
by John Martin

like the pain
in members amputated
thoughts run counter to the facts.

i sing
of seas long since dry
hunt old fruit
under apple trees
feel spring in winter's
brassy blasts
and apple blossoms
where old memories lie.

where memories lie
distorting now as liars will
and yesterday.

like pain
in legs no longer
there
and still they run
now not to hide, but find.

The yellow rose

27

Socrates

After making the rounds of the pet shop and not seeing any puppy that appealed to me, I approached the woman behind the counter. "Will you be having any more bearded collies, or part beardies?" I asked. My heart was still set on the bearded collie puppies I had seen three months prior in the store before I had left for vacation.

"Well, the brother of that dog you liked is still here—in the back," answered the shopkeeper who apparently remembered me. I didn't think she was right, because I had carefully looked throughout the store. "Really? I'll look again."

Way in the very back of the store, underneath a table with sign that read "Special Sale Only $60," I found a scraggly, no longer cute puppy dog. Had this dog been waiting for me?

A shop attendant brought the dog up to the front of the shop so I could look at him. The dog was homely and skittish; he had been fenced in and caged far too long. But even though frightened, he was very lovable.

"I found a dog!" I said to my husband over the telephone. "Can you come right away?"

While waiting I asked how old the puppy was. "He was born December 24th."

"Christmas Eve?" He was almost six months old. "Yes. December 24th."

A Christmas dog! Great qualifications. I wanted him.

Don had owned a collie as a child, and this dog was in the collie family. As soon as Don came and started petting the dog, I knew that even though he was acting cautious, he liked him too.

Soon we were in the car heading back home to Evanston, the frightened puppy slobbering all over my lap. Nothing I could do reassured him. I tried to calm him as Don and I discussed his name. Don would have liked to call him "Pal," but I wanted something more sophisticated. He suggested "Socs" because his four white feet looked like socks, but "Socs" was not an acceptable name for a dog born on Christmas Eve. I suggested "Socrates," inspired by my days at Shimer. Don agreed.

Socrates shook with fear all the way home to Evanston. Who knows why, but all his life, Socrates remained afraid of cars and vomited whenever we took him in the car. Likely, he was taken from his mother too young and then separated from his brother.

When we arrived home, little Socrates was very fearful and would not go up or down stairs and was afraid to go outdoors. Gradually he became braver.

A couple of months later, we moved to the Michigan UP (Upper Peninsula) to greet the new millennium. After Don's heart surgery, Socrates became his exercise program, and for the next ten years, they walked two miles together each morning.

When I joined Don in Trout Creek at the end of the year, I also became close with Socrates. He would sit with me on the sofa while I had my morning coffee. Socrates grew into a beautiful dog and looked a lot like the shaggy dog in the movies. I loved to pet his long beautiful hair. Sometimes Socrates would sit so he blocked my view of the TV, at which times it was I who would finally move. He often put his butt on my lap when I petted him. Trainers say not to allow that, but I liked having him on my lap.

When I walked Socrates, he would stop to watch a car coming; he was waiting to see if it were someone who would give him treats. Nancy, and Fred, formerly the town constable when the town had a constable, were Socrates's best friends and also Lorri, who came to visit from Chicago and loved to take him for long, long walks. Socrates liked to stop and roll in the grass, or if it were winter, to roll in the snow. His fur looked especially beautiful when it was covered with snowy white frost.

Socrates also helped around the house. He would clean and lick dishes for me before they went into the dishwasher. When he got the last of a butter or margarine container, he would pick it up with his teeth and take it into the dining room as if he knew it was sufficiently gourmet to be eaten in a more formal setting.

In the evening, Socrates would go to Don around 8:30, sit directly in front of him, and look squarely at Don until Don laughed. "Walk, Socrates?" one of us asked, and Socrates would bark. Around 9:30 or 10:00 p.m., Socrates would quietly, without saying a bark to either of us, go upstairs to bed. He slept on the queen-size bed in the guest room, which I kept covered with a wool blanket. Usually, I would come in before I went to bed and tell him good night.

Like a musical assistant, Socrates announced my piano students when they came to the door (and everyone else too). He was good at greeting visitors, and while he didn't care very much for toys, he would always pick up a ball, a neglected toy, or even a bone and bring it to a visitor as if making an offering. But as soon as the person reached for the rope-toy or stringy stuffed animal, he would quickly turn away. He played "keep away" with humans, not "fetch."

I loved the way Socrates responded to music. When I was giving a piano lesson, he would lie in front of the piano bench, contentedly listening, unless it was dissonant music or a student was not playing well, in which case he would get up and leave. Critic! He also loved to listen to classical music. Mozart was his favorite, and he would lie listening in front of the speakers, completely content.

When he wanted to go out and I was busy at the computer, Socrates would paw my arm so that I couldn't use the computer until I got up and took him for a walk. Sometimes I could get him to wait until I finished a paragraph or page. If I didn't take too long, Socrates would be patient, which I appreciated.

My loud sneezes alarmed Socrates, and if I sneezed downstairs, he would come rushing down like an emergency tech. When "Soco" came back from a walk, he would sit on the porch or on the sidewalk watching the world go by. He especially liked to do that on very clear nights. Rarely did he seem to mind the cold, unless snow got stuck between his toes.

His long black, gray, and white coat made him unusually handsome, but nothing was more captivating than his soulful brown eyes. Socrates's gaze was one of love, trust, and awareness. He seemed to sense if I were sad, and he would comfort me by kissing me on my cheek.

He hardly ever ran away, but when he did, he ran right over to our friends and neighbors: a lively old Polish woman, Sophie, and her daughter Wanda. Sometimes on a walk, he pulled on the leash to go and visit them, because he knew they would give him some delicious leftovers, or perhaps he could steal some cat food.

Sometimes, Socrates got the crazies. He would bark, then start running in circles through the house. "What's wrong with him?" a visitor would ask as Socrates ran past him like a comet and up the hallway stairs or "Is he all right?" as Socrates came tear-ing down the stairs and circled again through the house while I yelled, "Stop it! Stop it, Socrates!" But Socrates kept circling from the music room, through the dining room, out into the kitchen, back into the music room, then into living room again. *No one* could stop Socrates when he had the crazies. If he got them while outside, he would dash all over the yard in circles, around the house, into the neighbor's yard, and repeat the whole thing again and again.

If I woke up in the middle of the night and couldn't sleep, or if Don were snoring and I couldn't get back to sleep, I'd crawl in beside Socrates in the guest room. He was gracious and moved over, but if I moved around too much, he would get off the bed and lie on the rug next to the bed. I would say, "You don't have to go, Socrates. Stay." But Socrates knew how to care for himself as well as others.

Our friend and house sitter, Liisa, took care of him and stayed with him when we were gone. She loved him dearly, and Socrates felt the same way about her. He would mope big time when we or Liisa left. She felt so bad that she arranged to have her bag picked up so Socrates couldn't see her leave our house with it and be depressed. But as sad as he was for Liisa to leave, Socrates was always glad to see us and vice versa. He would be at the window looking out when we came and would bark and wag his tail. We would pet him and say how glad we were to see him; then he would go to the kitchen to eat and drink. Socrates would never eat or drink while left alone.

Socrates seemed to know when one of us was coming home and from what direction. Don would see Socrates at the south window in the living room several minutes before I drove in from that direction. Socrates also liked to sit on the stairs; we could see his image through the stained glass window at the stair landing when we drove in the driveway..

Bad habits. Socrates liked to eat deer poop and hated riding in cars. He seemed to think the vacuum cleaner was a dog-eating dragon. He liked to roll in animal-smelling grass and would get so stinky he needed a bath, which he hated.

But Socrates had his principles. He would turn his nose up to a cookie if he felt it were a bribe. If we offered a dog cookie before we left on a trip, he knew we were just mollifying him. He would not accept bribes. Socrates was an amazing dog!

We taught him several dog tricks when he was still a puppy—shake right paw, left paw, lie down, stay. Socrates was very smart, and we could have trained him better than we did, but we liked him the way he was, and taking him to a trainer would mean more car rides.

I loved to walk or sit with Socrates next to Lake Superior near our log home. I saturated my feet with the cold water of the vast magnificent lake while he walked on the sand. He didn't like to walk *in* the lake—he was afraid of the waves, but he enjoyed getting his paws wet or drinking water when the water was still. He loved to drink out of mud puddles and seemed to find them as delicious as fine teas.

When we were out by the lake, Socrates would go down to the waterfront and investigate—look out at the water, sniff around the shore as if he were on the edge of the world. Between the lake and the cabin, he would run and run, circling—perhaps around imaginary sheep. Don or I would call, "Come! Socrates, Come!" And Socrates would come running like the cavalry in motion!

* * * * *

In January of Socrates's eleventh year, we were at the cabin. Before we left, I wanted to snowshoe out to the lake, and Socrates came along. He seemed fine, but he lingered at the lake. On the way home, we stopped at the vet because Socrates had a cough, and we learned that Socrates's health was more fragile than we realized. Dr. Sturmer detected a heart problem and prescribed a beta blocker and water pills. On Monday, we brought him back. The beta blocker wasn't working. Socrates needed to see a specialist as soon as possible, and Dr. Sturmer made an appointment for him the next day in Duluth. If we found the right medicine for his heart, Socrates could still have some good years.

That night when I went in to say good night, I bent down to tell him, "I need you to live a while longer if you possibly can." During the night, he came into our bedroom and lay at the foot of our bed. When I saw him in the morning, he seemed thinner, and he seemed afraid.

On Tuesday morning, we headed for Duluth with Socrates in the car, which I knew would be hard on him, 165 miles each way. We placed Socrates on a soft blue blanket in the hatchback so he could look out and also lie down. Before we left town, we stopped at the post office in our little town. Socrates was sitting in the hatchback looking out, and he saw his good friend Nancy, who had stopped behind us to mail a letter. She gave Socrates some cookies (though he wouldn't eat in the car). He and Nancy gazed at one another. They seemed to communicate at a level I was not privileged to understand. Later Nancy told me that Socrates had said to her, "I won't be back."

Halfway to Duluth, we stopped at the Bad River Casino gas station. While Don pumped gas, I would take Socrates for a short walk. When Socrates got out of the car, he had difficulty walking. He struggled, managed for a while, peed, and lay down in the snow.

"He won't get up!" I said to Don. "I'm really worried about him."

"I'll drive the car over to him." Don drove the car near where Socrates was lying down, picked him up, and placed him back in the hatchback. We still had eighty miles to go.

When we were fifteen or twenty miles away from the clinic, I heard Socrates make an odd unfamiliar sound; it sounded like a call. "Hurry. Hurry," I said.

"We're almost there," Don answered.

We parked outside the clinic, and both jumped out of the car to check on the dog. Don opened the hatchback. There, Socrates lay, on the soft blue blanket, his eyes wide open. He was dead.

"Socrates! Oh, no! No. No. No!"

Don took his pulse and then ran into the clinic. Two technicians came running out holding a stretcher.

Maybe he's in a coma, I thought.

But one of the technicians shook her head, "He's gone."

Don and I held each other as we stood by the car. We both wept. "Oh, no. Not when we just got him here!"

We went inside, where strangers kindly tried to console us. According to the doctor, Socrates had likely thrown a clot, had a heart attack, and died immediately. It was too bad. If only we had gotten there earlier! Now his body lay in the back of our car, and we had a 165-mile ride home. We went back to the car and opened the hatchback.

"I love you so much, Socrates," I said. My intense love for him was close to physical pain. Don looked at Socrates's body and made the same kind of mourning sounds as those I heard at the Wailing Wall in Jerusalem.

We placed the soft blue blanket over Socs. There was no reason to go home; Socrates would not be there waiting for us. But our vet *was* waiting for us in his office.

It may seem a strange thing to do, but we drove back to the Bad River Casino gas station, where I looked for where "Soco" had peed in the snowbank less than two hours before, but we could not find it. We tried to find the patch of snow where Socrates last lay down and together finally determined where we thought it was. Before we left the station parking lot, we opened the hatchback and held our hands palms upward and gave Socrates a blessing on his journey. Again we told him that we loved him very much and would miss him terribly. We sang the Hawaiian lullaby to him, climbed into the car, and continued driving for another hour and a half.

As we drove, we talked about the unwavering, unconditional love Socrates gave so freely, how the love he gave Don was different from the love he gave me. He and Don shared a cooperative, buddy type of love. He was Don's pal, and Don's personal trainer, who had accompanied him on walks each morning in rain, snow, sleet, and sun, keeping Don's heart in his care for ten years. The love Socrates gave me was something different, a comforting love that said, "You are all right. Everything is all right. Life is good. We are in this together."

Socrates taught me a lot about what life is. Life is running through grass and feeling the wind flow through your hair or coat; it is about walking on the beach with the water and sand encircling your toes; it is listening to the crunch of the snow under our feet and paws, looking out at the stars on a winter night with the cold wind blowing on our faces. It is the signal of a paw on my arm. It is experiencing physical, emotional, and spiritual touch when all are one.

The day Socrates died, I didn't care about accomplishing goals or certainly not about having stuff or for a while, even about eating food. I only cared about the deep, understanding love that had no words.

Socrates gave so much enjoyment and love to many people and asked for very little in return. The vet, who had not known him very long, said, "He had a presence. That dog made a statement." He was exactly right. Socrates had a presence; he made a statement. Because I felt I had not fully recognized this Buddha-like presence that had been living with me, helping us every day for ten years, I mourned him deeply. I wasn't grateful enough.

Now he was gone, Socrates, my sweetheart dog. I understand he had to go. It was his time; I just wasn't ready. But Socrates is as much part of a divine plan as anyone. Yes, you, Socrates.

My grief over Socrates's death touched off other latent deep pools of grief that I did not understand. Two days following Socrates's life-ending, I left for Seattle, Washington, to attend a "breathing" workshop. There I was able to fully express and work through more grief.

I now view all animals differently than I did before Socrates lived with us. I have a greater reverence for life in all forms. I no longer believe that only human beings are spiritual beings. God's creation includes much more.

* * * * *

Two months after Socrates's life-ending, we adopted Barclay, a beautiful full-blooded rescue bearded collie. We were told he had separation anxiety, and for two months, we never left him alone in the house. Barclay still hates to be left alone, and he comes with us whenever possible.

Barclay shares many of Socrates's peculiar behaviors—the way he likes an appetizer before eating his dog food and how he waits at the window looking for us when we come home. He greets us with even more enthusiasm than Socrates did, but fortunately, he is also very different. Barclay *loves* cars. He, in fact, has an obsession about them and never vomits in them. Instead, he barks like he's herding sheep and turns a pirouette in the car when we meet a big truck. Also, he *loves* toys and wants to play endlessly with them—Socrates thought toys were beneath him. Barclay insists we play with him. But just like Socrates, Barclay is much more interested in playing "keep away" than playing "fetch."

Barclay is definitely his own dog and although ten years old, still acts like a puppy. He doesn't have Socrates's wise ancient presence of spirit, which we still miss, but he possesses a rare eagerness, a demand for involvement in life that's inspiring! I would like to do something as much as Barclay wants to have a walk, ride in the car, or greet the garbage truck.

* * * * *

In June, the year Socrates died, we had an open house/memorial service for sixteen of Socrates's closest friends. We ate ice cream sundaes, shared memories, and buried Socrates's ashes under the pine tree in what passes for our annual flower garden. Again, we sang the Hawaiian lullaby to him.

Barclay was not feeling well at the time; he had just been diagnosed with Addison's disease. That too has been a journey, and we are doing well with it. We love Barclay for his own ways of being. A rescue dog, it seems Barclay has rescued us as much as we rescued him. Life seems to provide rescuing services on a fairly regular basis.

Recently, the question was asked of me, what would you do if you knew this was the last day you had to live? To my surprise, my first thought was, "I'd play ball with Barclay in the backyard." This was an unexpected response because playtime (which Barclay comes and demands daily) often feels like an imposition. He doesn't play fair, and I get very annoyed with him because I rarely get the ball. Why on earth would it be my first choice if I only had one day to live?

The answer? Because playing with the dog is such a wonderful, "earthly" thing to do! The dog. Running. The yard. The ball. Who knows when and where an opportunity like that will come again?

Barclay, want to play?

Socrates

AFTERWORD

In 2013, we moved to Rocky Shores, our cottage where each morning I could look out and greet our magnificent Lake Superior in this incredible creation we call earth. The lake is vast, and it is new and different every day. Sometimes the lake is roaring; other times it is nearly inaudible. Waves may be huge and destructive or hardly a ripple. Each new day, each nanosecond, the lake is unlike it is any other nanosecond.

The world is beautiful and peaceful there, so much so that I now understand why Adam and Eve had to bring in the Apple Crisis. Not that it was right, but it may have been necessary for us to appreciate Eden. It took me more than a year to adjust to the new natural rhythm, the lack of diversions from diversions, to become more aware of what has always been true: all my obligations are home-made.

Each day is extraordinary because it is happening in the now—I wake, sleep, walk, sit, work, play, cry, laugh, love—I want to gather my life up, hug and kiss it, tell it how much I love it, and ask it not to leave me.

But like one of the stories in this book, my life will be over soon! That will be that! But with all my heart and soul, I knew it does not end there. Many people believe that people must be saved before death or they will go somewhere unpleasant afterward, but the opposite is much more likely. I believe opportunities for growth continue after life ends: we can expect to go from awareness to knowledge, from goodness to grace, from understanding to more clarity, from happiness to joyousness.

As for the here and how, life keeps unfolding—with surprises. After five years living each day enjoying Lake Superior, the Porcupine Mountains, and many good friends, we received an unexpected invitation from my niece, Thais, inviting us to come to New Mexico to oversee my great nephew Aidan's senior year in high school (also care for two dogs, Angel and Jo Jo) so she could accept a job in Washington, D.C. It seemed timely and right for us to do so. Seven months in Albuquerque brought a new way of life and we moved away from our beloved Rocky Shores in October 2018. A new adventure! We left our beloved Rocky Shores—the lake, the forest, and the wilderness, and moved to the desert, the mountains, and the city.

Each life is a work of art, a self-painting inspired by soul knowledge, life experiences and guided by the universal God. Sometimes at times of death, as well as other times, we have an opportunity to see the eternity connection between the here and the hereafter.

Tell your stories, create your spiritual legacy, and if you wish to do so, contact me through my website: www.joyibsen.com.

> Where God's Spirit is the rudder
> And His Word the compass true,
> as in fairy-tales the hour glass
> of eternity runs true;
> straightway without trial or wait,
> opens the eternal gate.[1]
>
> N. F. S. Grundtvig

ACKNOWLEDGMENTS

What a journey! In *Here and Hereafter*, I traveled to distant childhood memories and revisited experiences of the eternal. I would not have been able to publish this book without loving help along the way.

To Don Lenef, my loving husband for his unswerving support, encouragement, patience, and candid assessments. He is a brave man!

My children: Thea Martin for her perception, independent thinking, uncanny insight, and commitment to excellence; to Mitch Martin for his writing, teaching, and language expertise, for being as wonderfully encouraging to his mom as he is to his children and his students; and to Noah Martin for his knowledge of internet marketing, wisdom, and spot-on, right-to-the-core advice.

To my sister Karma Ibsen and my late brother David Ibsen for their reinforcement, for sharing remembrances and cheering me on with ideas and suggestions. I'm glad we share the same parents.

To Lars Clausen for guiding me with incredible patience, uncanny perceptions, expertise, and ever-ready assistance. It is a pleasure to work with a fellow Grundtvigian!

To Gary Vitale, a superb writer and actor who has experienced deep grief, for his writing expertise, careful review, and his honest and profound questions leading to increased clarity or greater depth.

To Jeannie Manning, one of my spirit sisters, a lay minister and retired policewoman, for her helpful comments and questions.

To Bruce Johansen, Janet Jensen, Ann Becker and Edward Broadbridge, for their thoughtful proofreading. What a team!

To Megan McGeowin, for rejecting my doubting.

To Judy Bruno, Lucy McDonald, and Lorri Wirsum, fellow writers in the Trout Creek Library Writers' Group who listened, commented, critiqued, wept, and laughed with me over early drafts of several of these stories.

Last and first of all, my grateful thanks to the Stratton Press team: Jeff Reid, Kobe Williams, and Angela James for their assistance in creating this new version of *Here and Hereafter: The Eternity Connection*. It would not have happened without them!

Thank you! I love you all!

Joy Ibsen

ABOUT THE AUTHOR

Joy Ibsen and her husband, Don Lenef, live in sunny urban Albuquerque, New Mexico, having moved in 2018 from Michigan's Upper Peninsula, where they lived on the shores of Lake Superior next to Porcupine Mountain State Park. They previously resided in Trout Creek, Michigan, and Evanston, Illinois. The couple have five children and five grandchildren between them.

Joy has three other published books: *Songs of Denmark: Songs to Live by; Unafraid, Life Lessons: Sermons to live By and Tales of Listeners learning to Live Unafraid*, coauthored by her father, Harald Ibsen; and *Poetry in the Porkies* from a workshop taught by Joy in the Porcupine Mountains.

Joy grew up in Danish American communities in Minnesota, Iowa, and South Dakota and has a passion for the work of N. F. S. Grundtvig, the Danish theologian, politician, educator, poet, and hymn writer, now recognized as a nation-builder. She was editor of the only Grundtvigian journal in the United States, *Church and Life*, for fourteen years, ending in December 2019. In 2013 Joy spent two months in Denmark studying Grundtvig's current relevance to modern life by interviewing thirty-two Danish citizens.

She graduated from high school in Viborg, South Dakota, attended Grand View University in Des Moines, Iowa, graduated from Shimer College then in Mount Carroll, Illinois, and pursued graduate studies at the University of Chicago Divinity School, where she had two classes with theologian Paul Tillich. She has a certificate in Lay Ministry from the School of Theology, University of the South.

Her varied career includes serving as a caseworker for public aid recipients in Chicago's Woodlawn ghetto; teaching GED to Vietnam-bound soldiers at Fifth Army Headquarters, Chicago; teaching English literature and theater to students at St. Katherine's/St. Mark's preparatory school in Davenport, Iowa; serving as chief planner for the Model Cities Program in Rock Island, Illinois; fund raising and management consulting for community, education, and art organizations; and heading development offices at Mount Sinai, Methodist, and Swedish Covenant hospitals in Chicago. In the Upper Peninsula, she taught piano lessons and served as church organist.

NOTES

NOTES TO CHAPTER 11

1. *King Came Preaching: The Pulpit Power of Dr. Martin Luther King JR.*, by Mervyn A. Warren & Gardner C. Taylor, InterVarsity Press, 2008, ISBN 083083253X, pg 174.
2. Pilkington, Ed (2008-04-03). "40 years after King's death, Jackson hails first steps into promised land," London: The Guardian.http://www.guardian.co.uk/ world/2008/apr/03/usa.race.

NOTES TO CHAPTER 16

1. "That Cause can never be lost nor stayed" (Verse 1) by Kristian Ostergaard, translated by J. C. Aaberg.
2. "O Land of Our King" (Verse 1) by N. F. S. Grundtvig, translated by S. D. Rodholm.

NOTES TO CHAPTER 17

1. *You Can Heal Your Life*, Louise Hay, Hay House, Inc., 26th printing, 2008, page 184.

NOTES TO CHAPTER 24

1. "Evening Star" (First and last verses) by Chr. Richardt, 1861, translated by S. D. Rodholm.

NOTES TO THE AFTERWORD

1. "Old enough have I become now," verse 4 of N.F.S. Grundtvig's last poem, translated by Edward Broadbridge.